The Doctor's Death Diagnosis

Self Care, Your Health, And Healing Secrets

Edward Palmer

The Doctor's Death Diagnosis

The Doctor's Death Diagnosis

*Self Care, Your Health,
And Healing Secrets*

Edward G. Palmer

Publisher:

JVED Publishing
13570 Grove Drive #361
Maple Grove MN 55311
http://www.jvedpublishing.org

Print Edition
ISBN-13: 978-0976-883395
All Rights Reserved

For everyone who wants a longer healthier life,
And, especially for those with a doctor's death diagnosis.

Table Of Contents

A special thanks to my wife Becky for her creative thoughts, editorial inputs, and encouragement.

CHAPTER ONE
Introduction

When a friend, who I'll call Jane, entered the room and announced that she had been diagnosed with ALS (Amyotrophic lateral sclerosis, aka Lou Gehrig's disease), my mind started racing. ALS is a cruel doctor's death diagnosis and involves eventually losing control of the muscles throughout the body. It might initially manifest as the weakness or loss of total control over one leg or arm and ultimately result in the inability to swallow. Pain is usually involved in disease progression, and life expectancy is often only two years after diagnosis.

My first thought was, what do doctors and allopathic[1] medicine know about ALS? This came to my mind first because doctors have a limited knowledge base, and this was not the first death diagnosis I had heard. The knowledge base of doctors is mainly limited to standard medical practices, and continuing education is supplied by industry forces like large pharmaceutical companies. Keeping up with the latest in drug treatment information is a massive task in and of itself. Doctors who stray from standard medical practices can face expensive negligence lawsuits and even lose their medical licenses.

Medical doctors' education is severely limited regarding nutrients and nutraceuticals (vitamins, herbs, etc.) and alternative health approaches to healing. This is especially true when it comes to the use of mega doses of vitamins and nutrition (Orthomolecular Medicine[2]). This field of medicine seeks to treat disease through nutritional supplementation, including mega nutrient doses. Giving the body what it needs in the form of nutrients and at an amount that is productive for healing.

When you go to a medical doctor, you should realize you are in their medical specialty and within their knowledge base constraints. Inherently this means that the effects of nutrients on the human body may not be within their expertise. You'll need to go to a Naturopath[3] or a nutritional expert to understand how nutrients impact the human body. Otherwise, you'll need to find alternative doctors or study nutrient approaches to disease and healing for yourself[4].

Think about this reality. If a small aspirin tablet can reduce pain, why wouldn't other natural nutrients[5] also work? All doctors admit that severe Vitamin C deficiency can cause scurvy in humans. However, what other conditions could benefit from Vitamin C? Did you know that Vitamin C in large doses can kill viruses like the

COVID-19 coronavirus circulating throughout the world in 2020-2022? Did you realize Vitamin C[6] in large amounts can also kill cancer cells[7]?

Medical doctors, for the most part, have limited knowledge of nutraceuticals unless they have transitioned to the field of alternative medicine. A list of alternative doctors and websites I recommend is included in the last chapter on "Healing Secrets & Tips."

It gets worse when it comes to medical information. Knowledge is now increasing at a phenomenal rate. Medical doctors are struggling just to keep up with the advances in their own areas of healthcare practice. It is difficult to find a general practitioner (GP) in the medical industry today. The industry is too subdivided into specialty healthcare practices.

There are over 20 significant specialties with many sub-specialties within those categories, leading to hundreds of specific professions in allopathic medicine. Think of surgery as a meaningful category in the medical field. You will find rectal surgery, general surgery, plastic surgery, hand surgery, neurological surgery, ophthalmic surgery, pediatric surgery, vascular surgery, and many other surgical subclasses within this specialty. Get the picture?

Knowledge has expanded to the point where a career as a general practitioner found in the 1950s is no longer possible in the 21st century. Information is too massive, which is why the vocation of "Doctor" is now broken down into many specialties. Suppose you go to a clinic for an ear problem. In that case, you will likely get referred to another doctor, an ear medical specialist, or an ear clinic. Think about any part of the human body. Odds are high that a medical doctor or clinic specializing in that particular body part already exists.

Suppose you spend 12-20 hours on Internet research. In that case, you might be more educated and current about your health issue or disease than the doctor you plan to see. We are all pressed for time to keep up with unfolding events and new education. Medical doctors are no exception. You can apply this knowledge to almost any field. It certainly applies to my area of electrical engineering, which I entered over 50 years ago. And it was part of a Prophecy thousands of years ago.

"But you, Daniel, shut up the words and
seal the book until the time of the end;
many shall run to and fro, and knowledge
shall increase." Daniel 12:4 (NKJV)

When I heard about Jane's ALS diagnosis, the limited healing knowledge base of medical doctors crossed my mind. A doctor's death diagnosis normally doesn't consider healing aspects outside standard allopathic medicine (drugs, chemotherapy, radiation, surgery, or other medical practices). This means that nutrition, nutrient, and megavitamin approaches to healing are not even under consideration by most doctors.

The second thought that ran through my mind was how people usually take the doctor's diagnosis to heart. We have been taught that doctors are always right. I've even read that doctors are trained to act as the final authoritative word when giving patients health directives. If this was Jane's state of mind, she might resign to letting ALS take its natural course on the body. Of course, the doctor would offer palliative care to minimize pain, etc.

I would challenge the doctor's death diagnosis. This can be done by researching the disease and other alternative healing modalities. At age 76, I understand that opinions are the cheapest commodity in the world. Everyone's got one, including medical doctors and all their death diagnoses.

It's a fact. There is a massive Internet knowledge base for disease and alternative healing research. These are areas you can mine in your death diagnosis offensive for healing your body instead of accepting death. In this regard, I'll explain what I've learned over the last 50 years of my life.

None of the contents of this book are meant to disparage the profession of medical doctors. I only seek to point out their limited knowledge of how nutrients and nutraceuticals can heal your body. If you have received a doctor's death diagnosis, you must take charge of your health care. At the least, find a doctor that has alternative healing options available for you to consider.

Recently another friend asked me: "Don't most doctors have big hearts and really care?" My answer to him was:

"I would think so. However, a doctor's education and medical treatment modalities are tightly controlled. Suppose you add the limited knowledge of nutrition and nutraceuticals. In that case, you have a minimal and expensive approach to treating symptoms instead of curing the underlying health condition.

A perfect illustration exists in suppressing Vitamin C usage as a therapy for killing viruses and even curing cancer. Finding a doctor in the United States who will administer Vitamin C intravenously is difficult. In contrast, in Shanghai[8], China, doctors recognize Vitamin C as a viable treatment for the COVID-19 disease caused by the SARS-CoV-2 novel coronavirus. Bottom line? It revolves around money and Big Pharma controlling medical treatment options in pursuit of wealth & power.

Big hearts and caring will only get you so far in today's

fragmented healthcare system. Odds are high that the doctor's big heart and caring will get you sent to a specialist in the treatment of your illness or medical needs." From there, you'll face standard medical practices and the limitations of Big Pharma-controlled conventional allopathic medicine. Think drugs!

Allopathic doctors and medicine may provide you with a convincing set of facts. You need to know the alternative healing side to the health care story for healing your body. You'll find nutrients, nutraceuticals, and other alternative ways to improve your body's health in the pages of this book.

It was with a sad heart over my friend's ALS death diagnosis that inspired me to tell you my story of how I've used alternative approaches to health for the last 50 years. I recently learned about orthomolecular medicine and its megavitamin doses to cure disease. This area of medicine has expanded my understanding of how to use nutraceuticals.

In this book, I will focus on using my experiences' with nutrients and nutraceuticals. However, I will also explain what orthomolecular medicine means for your health and the abundance of available resources.

You'll learn why and how I usually steer clear of doctors and hospitals. You'll learn alternative healing strategies and why traditional doctors might not tell you about them, even if they knew them.

Some Definitions

Before we go further, let me define a few terms for you that I will be using in this book.

Allopathic medicine means traditional medicine and its standardized medical practices using pharmaceutical drugs, chemotherapy, radiation, surgery, etc. Allopathic medical practices focus on the suppression of symptoms using drugs, surgeries, and other modalities instead of the underlying causes of sickness or disease.

Naturopathic medicine means doctors who diagnose, treat, and manage patients with acute and chronic conditions while addressing disease and dysfunction at the level of body, mind, and spirit. A naturopath doctor attempts to treat the entire individual, understanding that emotional and spiritual problems may be part of the disease.

Integrative medicine combines standard medical practices with complementary approaches to maximize healing for those with chronic or complex health issues.

This would include chiropractic care, yoga, and meditation.

Functional medicine means a systems biology-based approach (via testing) that focuses on identifying and addressing the root cause of disease. In this regard, it is similar to integrated medicine in that it seeks to broaden standard medical care practices to include more modalities. Blood and other testing are a new method of determining your body's nutrient needs. In the future, blood tests will be used to optimize vitamin needs, thereby taking the guessing out of swallowing nutraceutical pills. This will be a welcomed relief for many who consume a lot of nutraceuticals like me.

Electroceutical medicine uses energy technology devices and frequencies to diagnose and treat disease.

Alternative medicine means any health or healing modality not part of standardized medical practices used by allopathic, conventional, or traditional medicine.

Nutrition means food.

Nutraceuticals include vitamins, herbs, and specialty

supplement formulations (Eye Health, Heart Health, Diabetes Support, etc.).

Nutrients mean food or nutraceuticals.

Orthomolecular medicine means mega doses of nutrition and vitamins, as determined by your body's requirements. The essence of this approach is to feed your body the nutrients it needs in the quantity it needs for effective healing.

Supplements are another word for nutrients or nutraceuticals.

Self-Care means anything that you can do for yourself that will improve your body's health. This includes health studies or seeking advice from any type of health professional.

Edward G. Palmer, Author

———

CHAPTER TWO
A Doctor's Death Diagnosis

DEATH IS NO STRANGER TO ME

"To everything, there is a season ...
A time to be born
And a time to die
And a time to heal."
Ecclesiastes 3:1-3 (NKJV)

Death has always been a part of my experience of living. I suspect death is also an experience in your life. Unfortunately, the older you get, the more exposure to death you get. I know the lucky ones have been spared the terrible experience of losing a mother, father, brother, sister, or other close loved one to death.

The first significant death in my life occurred at the age of 13. This was when my father died in Minneapolis. The year was 1959. He fell down two flights of steps and died from a brain injury after lying unconscious in the Hennepin County's General Hospital for 52 days. He never regained consciousness after the accident.

It was the direct result of alcohol consumption and the celebration of our new apartment home in the projects of North Minneapolis. My father had a French-Canadian heritage. He was a tremendous influence on my life. To the extent I can display any ability to love and to be kind, I will give him credit for the love and kindness he showed me during the formative years of my youth (12<).

One of his tricks to show how much he loved me was to tell me he had a secret to share with me, but he needed to whisper it into my ear. When I leaned over to hear, he grabbed me so I couldn't leave. Then he smooched me with a lot of kisses and tickled me. I've pulled the same routine on my own kids and grandkids. I have to believe my grandfather pulled it on him first.

When my father died, my mother, who was German and more stoic and less emotional, told me, "big boys don't cry." I was not allowed to fully grieve my father's death. Eventually, I dealt with it, but at this moment, I had officially entered the "Male's Emotional Box."

Ever wondered why most males have trouble sharing their feelings? Maybe it is because parents or other family members have forced them to bottle up their emotions, putting them into a male or man emotional box. At age 21, I broke the mold and allowed myself to feel and express my feelings. The story of this death trauma is continued in another chapter.

I mention it here because suppressing trauma like this can result in severe sickness and disease later in life. If you find yourself in an unexplainable illness or cancer, start searching your past for trauma "boxed" up and deep inside your subconscious mind. Believe it or not, what's buried in the depths of your mind can surface and create havoc for your health. In the "Anatomy Of A Health Crisis," I tell the story of how this happened to me.

At the same time my father died, his parents suddenly disappeared from my life. I was told they both died, but I wasn't allowed to attend their funerals or say goodbye. I'm not sure how this affected my youth, but by age 15, I was living away from my mother and drinking a quart of booze every week. The love of a woman and God's grace allowed me to move forward with a healthier lifestyle.

My first son, Glenn, died at five weeks of age in 1965 while my wife and I were driving across the country to my Navy ship in Long Beach, CA. The coroner said it was SIDS. If it was, it could have been caused by our cigarette smoking in the car. My wife and I were both smokers at that time. In those days, we still saw cigarette ads that proclaimed smoking was healthy for us. Yet, from what I have learned and now understand about vaccines and their neurotoxins, I'd lean more towards the belief that the vaccines the baby received before going on our trip were a more probable cause.

That death was traumatic for a 19-year-old male (me) and his 18-year-old wife. Then there was the incredibly insensitive remark my wife's aunt made at the baby's Minneapolis funeral: "Don't worry, you're young. You can still have another!"

Death always arrives with a lot of fear, tears, troubles, and even controversies. Yet, death is a part of living and cannot be avoided.

At age 21, my mother was the next to pass away. She suffered from polio and then multiple sclerosis. The last time I visited her, she had lost control of almost every body part, including her eyes. This was when my wife and I were traveling back to Minneapolis, with our new baby girl, on leave from the Navy. We stopped to visit with her in Kennewick, Washington, where she was living with my stepfather. I knew she wasn't going to live long. That much was evident from her physical condition. The time spent visiting, however, allowed me to let her know I loved her. She was at least able to see her first granddaughter before she died.

We often find our human bodies living with a sickness or disease that the medical system can't fix. This was true of both my father and my mother. My father almost died of rheumatic fever when he was seven years old. It left him with grand mall seizures all his life. For many years, I thought he had epilepsy. An aunt told me the truth. You never could tell when an episode would strike, but when one started, you could tell by the darkness in his eyes. My father was a musician who played a dozen or more musical instruments. He composed the "Minneapolis Waltz" at the age of 21 in 1934, which he copyrighted. I obtained a copy of it from the Library of Congress.

For a while, he had his own band in Minneapolis. Yet the seizures and a stubborn non-union independence streak caused employment problems in the 40s and 50s. This was a time for musician unions. No membership, no jobs playing musical instruments.

My mother's health problems started as polio and then became MS. Both of my parents suffered. However, I cannot recall a single instance of them ever complaining about life. Suffering was always a part of their lives. It has also been a part of my and my family's life.

Many people in today's society expect miracles from the medical industry. I have come to believe that many people think they can do whatever they like in life. If a serious health event occurs because of their activities, the doctors can patch them up like new again. Really?

Death is no stranger to me. People die for many reasons, and it is tragic when they die young. I had a cousin whose son died at the age of 12. It was the saddest funeral I have ever attended. The boy was riding a motorcycle up a hill and, at the top, crashed and died. It really troubled my wife and me as our oldest daughter was the same age. Too often, we tend to project the misery we are exposed to onto our own families.

Some Deaths Close To Me

- My uncle Jack was sitting at a lake cabin table with two or maybe all three of his daughters when he closed his eyes. They thought he had fallen asleep. However, he had died instantly from a massive heart attack. Harsh on his daughters, but it seemed a peaceful and fast way of dying. No extended period of suffering. He just was gone.

- Cousin Dick died from alcohol in his mid-40s.

- Cousin John died from alcohol in his mid-40s.

- My sister died from surgery for obesity at 53.

- My first wife, Jackie, died of pancreatic cancer at 56. Her death diagnosis was as little as 10-14 days to live. She lasted 98 days. We were married 39 years and were high school sweethearts.

* * *

- Jackie's father died of colon cancer at 72. He suffered great pain and was emaciated at the end. We prayed for mercy for the last few months because his suffering and pain were too much to witness. He prolonged his suffering for three weeks to say goodbye to a granddaughter who was out of town.

- Jackie's mother died of a massive stroke at 73.

- My second father-in-law died of Alzheimer's at 94.

- My friend Vernon left the planet three days after he was told he would never walk again because of a spinal tumor. He was 82 when he just spiritually checked out.

- Death is no stranger to me. Nor is a doctor's death diagnosis a stranger to me. I'd like to live to 120. If I do, I will continue to suffer from losing people dear to me. The older you get, the more lives you'll see pass. I accept that reality in this life. Why would I like to live that long? I would like to see what a full Genesis 6:3 life contains. Yes, even though I know more suffering will come.

Some Lessons About Death

If you can't stop abusing drugs and alcohol, you can easily die in your mid-forties.

If you can't stop smoking cigarettes, you can easily die in your mid-50s or 60s.

Marijuana is not as innocent a drug as many people now believe. In a recent study, users were found to need emergency room services a complete 20% more than non-users. So logically, if you want fewer accidents, maybe don't use it?

If you can't stop bad habits, cancer or something just as serious usually catches up to you in your mid-fifties and takes you out in your early or mid-60s.

To live a long life, you must stop or reduce poor health habits and develop and adopt some healthy ones.

I believe my paternal grandparents living into their mid to upper 90s convinced me at a young age that I would live a long life. At least well into my 90s like they did. So thinking about longevity has always been with me. As a result of ditching some bad habits at a young age, I am hopeful of living a very long life.

I have to say I've had some help from God stopping bad habits. At age 14, I was hanging around with some bad company. These boys liked to steal cars and burgle homes. After a joy ride in a stolen car, we parked the car in an out-of-the-way place. Three days later, the car was still there, so the guys decided to retake it. I decided to part ways because this was not the life I wanted. Of course, the police had the car staked out, and the boys were arrested. This was a spiritual decision, and there is some ancient wisdom available.

"He who walks with wise men will be wise, But the companion of fools will be destroyed." Proverbs 13:20

The trauma of my father's death took a toll on me. I left home at age 15 and began drinking. I was an alcoholic at this young age, drinking one or more bottles of booze every week. Then, I ran into the love of my teen sweetheart, who told me she didn't want to see me again if I continued to drink all the time.

Love won out, and I dialed way back on the alcohol. Eventually, at age 32, I stopped drinking alcohol for good. I had an epiphany with God and did not want alcohol influencing my thoughts anymore. I had at that time been drinking 2-3 drinks a night. I sensed the influence of alcohol the next day on my thoughts. I wanted a clear mind to fully discern God's spirit in my life.

It's not that God isn't always there. He is. The problem with our modern lives is that we are so busy that there is no room for God. I was getting in tune with my spiritual side and needed to slow down. More ancient wisdom ...

"Be still, and know that I am God ..." Psalms 46:10

This literally means quieting the mind and body so you can hear and engage in a spiritual conversation.

Smoking was another issue for me that involved a lot of physical pain. I started smoking around age 10. My dad caught me at age 11. In his attempt to get me to stop, he sat me down in the living room and made me smoke one of his cigars. Unfortunately, after that, I also smoked cigars. Well, at least he tried. Sorry, Dad. It's on me! Still, a physical issue would come into play, eventually forcing me to quit. It was my sinuses. They have plagued me most of my life, especially in my youth.

It took a decade for me to quit smoking entirely at age 21. Every year as my smoking increased, I would get the proverbial smoker's cough which eventually got into my chest in the form of bronchitis. As I continued smoking, the pain would ratchet up directly with the number of cigarettes I consumed. By age 19, I was on to the connection and decided to quit smoking. Oops ... quitting smoking is not so easy a job.

I worked my way up to smoking three packs a day before being forced to slow down because of chest pain. I was a smoker of Pall Mall, Lucky Strike, and Camel cigarettes. The strongest available. Being in the Navy, I could buy cartons of cigarettes for $2.00 each while we were out past three miles. I decided to purchase menthol and other filtered brands to slow me down. This helped a little. I had just bought 20 cartons of awful cigarettes while out at sea. Back in port, I came aboard the ship and lit up a filtered Marlboro cigarette. After I inhaled the first drag, I started to cough uncontrollably. For ten minutes, it felt like a knife was being stuck in my chest and twisted. It was awful pain. I looked at the newly opened pack of cigarettes, then pitched it overboard and mentally proclaimed, "cigarettes are not worth that kind of pain." I was unsuccessful in trying to slow down until a final episode of pain allowed me to quit cold turkey. So while I failed with the mind, my body succeeded with its pain.

If I had some wisdom, I would have sold and gotten rid of those cigarette cartons. My wife wanted them, and

I was too young and dumb. She was never able to quit. When she stopped smoking in the house 25 years later, I gagged up black stuff from my lungs for quite a while. Nobody can convince me that secondhand smoke doesn't affect our bodies. However, when she died of pancreatic cancer in 2003, I discovered that smoking is an underlying cause of this cancer about 30% of the time.

When I quit, I thought for a moment that I wouldn't enjoy drinking at the time without smoking. This was naive on my part. I enjoyed drinking more because smoking actually ruins the taste buds. Everything started to taste better after I quit.

I never got into drugs but watched some shipmates who did. In 1970 on my last tour to Vietnam, the ship was infested with users of Marijuana. They offered it to me, but I refused. At the time, I was into scotch whiskey with Coca-Cola pop. One of the potheads threw away a small book on Marijuana that I picked out of the trash. It pointed out the behavioral issues involved, which I fully observed. Well, times have changed, and today's Marijuana is much more robust, and some of it is laced with Fentanyl, which can kill you. Nasty stuff.

In the early 70s, I was working on installing the first food scanners at Red Owl stores in Hopkins, MN. A sign in the manager's office of the Red Owl food center in Hopkins, stated some excellent advice for living.

THINK HABITS, CHANGE HABITS!

Suffering, pain, and death are built into our human existence. If we can avoid pain or illness, we are very fortunate indeed. However, I will point out that there is another side to healing that does not rely upon doctors. Instead, it involves taking responsibility for your health. Then, taking care of yourself and using nutrients, nutraceuticals, and other alternative modalities to keep yourself healthy throughout your life.

If you go on a self-care journey, you can find yourself guessing what ails you and what to take to fix yourself. Perhaps the least understood medical secret is that the doctor plays a guessing game also. He'll look at your symptoms and make the best guess he can of what is going on with your health. He may even order some tests to create a more educated guess, or he may just consult his Physician's Desk Reference (PDR) before prescribing a drug. So, in addition, to a typical 5-minute doctor consult and stiff bill, you will have entered the allopathic medicine's guessing game. At least one naturopath or functional doctor has stated her typical patient has already seen 13 doctors before getting to her. Some more ancient wisdom speaks directly to this complication in the medical system 2,000 years ago.

"Now a woman, having a flow of blood for twelve years, who had spent all her livelihood on physicians and could not be healed by any, came from behind and touched the border of his [Jesus'] garment. And immediately her flow of blood stopped." Luke 8:43-48 NKJV

Let's now begin a self-care journey by walking through the anatomy of a severe health care crisis of my own. Afterward, I'll review some key points you'll need to remember if you have to take a journey on your own. You don't have to take a doctor's death diagnosis as the final word. Alternative approaches to healing exist, and, yes, spontaneous healings do occur. I have seen them.

———

CHAPTER THREE
Anatomy Of A Health Crisis

A SERIOUS HEALTH ISSUE

A Self-Care Discussion & Approach
To A Serious Health Issue

I'll confess that I don't have all the answers to my current health issue. As I explain my thoughts on this health problem, I hope it will illustrate ways to approach self-care without undergoing expensive medical or dental treatments.

I also hope that it will give me some mental clarity on what I need to do to effect healing in my body.

The problem was a root canal infection that had eaten away the bone in my upper jaw that supported the tooth. This tooth was an anchor for a bridge that spanned one other tooth. I have a high-quality dentist whom I trust entirely. She had obtained an additional review of the x-rays. She had notified me in no uncertain terms that "the tooth was a goner and was probably already loose."

The implication was that the bone around and supporting the tooth would soon be gone. It would then become unstable or fall out of my upper jaw. The anchor securing one side of an attached bridge for one missing tooth would also become damaged or broken, with the tooth unstable or falling out.

The treatment plan was $6278 in cost. It involved removing the tooth, creating a temporary bridge, and allowing the jaw bone to heal for ten weeks. A permanent new bridge, spanning two missing teeth (instead of one), would be created after the jaw bone was given time to heal.

I had complete confidence in my dentist being able to do this work. She informed me that this would be the best strategy. An alternative fix would be to install an implant. However, this infected tooth goes into the sinus cavity. An implant might require sinus surgery first and possibly a bone graft. She also suggested I would not be a good candidate for an implant due to significant bone loss.

I told her I believed my body could get rid of the infection naturally and heal the bone surrounding the tooth. So, I decided I would give my self-care health protocols a chance to work before choosing a complicated and expensive dental procedure.

What's the worse case? I thought the tooth might fall

out as more bone got destroyed, leaving me with a mess in my mouth. According to a few sources, it could get complicated as the infection could spread and even get to my brain. It could even affect other parts of my body.

The video documentary "Root Cause," available online for free, identifies health problems from root canal surgeries. One stat cited was that over 90% of women with breast cancer have had a root canal on the same side as the breast with cancer. While a 90% correlation does not mean causation, it is a disturbing cancer statistic.

Maintaining dental health is very important. Doctors know that bad teeth or periodontal gum disease can result in heart attacks. Alternative doctors are also aware of various health conditions associated with mercury-based amalgam fillings in teeth. I had all the amalgam fillings removed from my teeth ten years ago. In their place are composite fillings. If I had known about the dangers of root canal procedures, I would have chosen an alternative. Of course, that assumes I could afford an alternative approach.

Dental repairs have become costly, and most insurance plans do not cover dental work beyond routine checks and cleaning. I have no valid medical or dental insurance except Medicare Part A. This senior benefit isn't much use without additional coverage. I have never used it once in the eleven years I have had Medicare Part A. If my body needs some medical care, it is an out-of-pocket cost for me, or it doesn't get done. It's that simple! Spiritually, I am ready to exit the planet if it comes to that, so the lack of basic medical insurance isn't stressful.

The connection between teeth and body organs is a new energetic health discovery. The blood vessels that feed the roots of our teeth are energetically connected to other body parts. As practiced by Chinese medicine, think of the body's energy meridians to fully understand this reality. If you search the Internet, you will find charts of how the teeth are associated with other body parts.

Our bodies are energy, now visible using infrared technology and accessible using energy-related instruments. Modern medicine is expanding into the new field of "Electroceuticals." This new field of alternative medicine can even treat sickness by treating the body's energy sources with micro-current frequencies. This energy technology is now about three decades old and sophisticated. Yet, most doctors know little about it. The Chinese have practiced energy-related medicine for centuries. Only recently can we see it, instrument it, and truly heal our bodies using electroceutical devices.

Choosing a root canal for a tooth can result in a severe medical issue. Many alternative doctors now suspect it could be a significant cause of unexplained, chronic, and mysterious illnesses. Add to that reality amalgam-filled teeth. Living with dead body parts or poisoning your body with known neurotoxins (mercury-based amalgam fillings) is not a good idea. Alternative, Integrated, and Naturopathic medical doctors would want to eliminate these teeth and gum problems from a healing perspective, especially if you are experiencing unexplainable or mysterious health symptoms.

Suppose you find yourself with the need for a root canal. In that case, you will benefit from first watching the "Root Cause" video documentary. A better choice than having a root canal procedure done would be removing the defective tooth and installing a non-metal implant. Do some research to save yourself a lot of grief, pain, and possibly a chronic, unexplainable future illness.

If you are dealing with a death diagnosis and have root canal teeth in your mouth, getting them removed may be the start of natural healing in your body. The issue of how dead teeth can affect the body energetically should be considered. Especially if your illness is unexplainable.

Getting 100% of the bacteria out of the tooth during a root canal surgery is almost impossible. The lingering bacteria cause recurring infections from the root canal procedure as long as the tooth remains in your jaw.

A family member had a similar issue and had the root canal tooth extracted. He was concerned and was the first to point out it could spread to the brain. My current wife was also concerned and didn't care if it cost $6278, even though this would be another burden on our budget.

I consider this health issue a gift from God to help me explain more thoughts about self-care for a severe health issue. I have practiced self-care alternative health protocols on my body for fifty-two years. I know my body wants to heal if I feed it the nutrients it needs and otherwise take care of myself.

The first lesson when using a self-care health approach is that family members might think you are playing Russian roulette with your health. "Why don't you just do what the doctor, or in this case, the dentist wants you to do?" You will need the courage to move forward with a self-care approach in the face of what the family might view as first being a safety issue. You will also need to listen to your gut. Take the time to get to know your body, how it feels, and how it reacts to health issues. Take the time to learn what you'll need to do to affect the healing your body needs.

Yes, it is very accurate that many people do not realize that the body wants to heal itself. This reality assumes you can get out of your own way and not do things that worsen your disease, illness, or healing needs.

Your body can eliminate infections. It can regrow bones, cartilage, and cells and otherwise repair itself.

Sayer Ji, the founder of GreenMedInfo.com, wrote an excellent book: "Regenerate: Unlocking Your Body's Radical Resilience Through The New Biology." It is a fantastic read that explains how your body can heal and why the body is meant to regenerate and heal itself. The new biology recognizes that the environment or terrain surrounding our body is more important than our genes.

Sayer Ji's website is an excellent place to research health issues. He has curated over 10,000 published health articles into a searchable database. While his website is membership-supported, his search function is available to the public. His newsletter is worth subscribing to, and he is connected to many leaders in the alternative health industry.

Natural antibiotics such as garlic can help you fight off bacterial infections. Here is a list of sixteen nutrients that function as natural antibiotics for the human body.

Natural Antibiotic Nutrients

1. Apple Cider Vinegar
2. Garlic
3. Ginger
4. Vitamin C
5. Olive Leaf Extract
6. Grapefruit Seed Extract
7. Horseradish Root

8. Habanero Peppers

9. Oregano Oil

10. Goldenseal

11. Echinacea

12. Turmeric

13. Raw Honey

14. Onion

15. Cinnamon

16. Iodine

These natural antibacterials fight against E. Coli or Salmonella, H. Pylori, ear infections, strep throat, wound infections, and other bacterial infections. These nutrients can be found on alternative health websites. Just use the search term: "natural antibiotics."

Get familiar with these natural antibiotics that the drug companies don't want you to know exist. Unlike prescription antibiotics, they don't kill off all bacteria in the body. Your gut needs good bacteria to function.

Suppose you are given a course of antibiotics. In that case, you need to know that the drug will kill both good and bad bacteria inside your gut (intestines). This is called your microbiome. There is a direct relationship between your gut microbiome's health and your body's overall health. This is why you will need to supplement with some probiotics afterward to rebuild the health of your gut.

You can access many online health resources to help you understand what you are up against regarding a disease, illness, and healing. I found some excellent images of root canal infections to help me understand the recovery I would need. In addition to image searching, you can search for items you think will help. I.E., the search for natural antibiotics. You can even search for how people beat the disease or illness you are up against.

Be aware that Google censors alternative health news and information about alternative health protocols or cures. Instead, they focus on standard practices in the allopathic medical industry as supported by the FDA, CDC, AMA, etc. They actively censor anything that contradicts traditional medicine supported by Big Pharma's drugs.

If you are reading this book, you may not benefit from searching inside the allopathic medical industry. You will probably want to explore alternative health websites and doctors, integrated doctors, naturopathic medicine, etc. You will also want to search for comments from others that struggle with the same illness or disease you have.

I use duckduckgo.com. This search engine does not censor alternative health news and reportedly does not keep track of your search activity. However, recent articles have disclosed anonymous search data is being sold to Microsoft, and some censoring is being done. Still, at the moment, I would recommend not using Google for its widespread censoring of alternative health solutions.

I use six items from the list of natural antibiotics regularly. The main natural antibiotic I am using is garlic 600 mg, two or more times a day. I also use ginger, Vitamin C, and turmeric daily. As the occasion requires, I also use Iodine and a product called OregaSpray on my throat and as a gargle. This oregano-based product can kill any germs in your throat and sinuses. It is one of the most amazing health products that I have discovered.

The first time I used oregano was with a product called Oregano Oil P70. After reading how it could clear the sinuses, I decided to use the product. I have had to contend with sinus issues my entire life. It works, but it has a terrible taste and almost gagged me.

The instructions recommended taking one drop under the tongue. I used two and found myself clutching my throat and wondering what I had done. It was a terrible experience, which reminded me of mothers in the 50s forcing children to take nasty-tasting cod liver oil for cold prevention in winters. In truth, I have no memory of my mother doing this, but it was a common occurrence in the days of my youth.

The nastiness lasted about 3-5 minutes, and then instant relief. Wow! I use the OregaSpray on the interior of my mouth and throat. It has the same initial result, a gagging feeling for 3-5 minutes and instant relief. I'm used to it now and consider it a miracle nutrient, an alternative health gift to kill off a virus or bacterial infection. I spray it on my throat (3-5 squirts) and then gargle with it before spitting it out. I get it into my sinuses by inhaling towards the roof of my mouth.

I had a bacterial infection in my upper jaw bone, and the need for a natural approach led me to these nutrients. I already knew about natural antibiotics. I had everything I was using on hand except the garlic. I've used these nutrients to enhance my immune system for years.

Now I began to test the effectiveness of self-care against a documented bacteria bone infection. After some thinking, I determined I had the following three root canal issues I needed to address to complete my healing.

1. Bacteria Infection
2. Inflammation
3. Bone loss

These issues led to additional research on natural antibiotics, anti-inflammation nutrients, and bone support.

Since my sinuses might be involved in my healing, I decided to use a Neti-Pot whenever my sinuses were acting up. A Neti-Pot can be found at Pharmacies and is used with water and salt to flush out the sinuses. The flush of the sinuses can be enhanced by using a drop of iodine or hydrogen peroxide. Both nutrients kill bacteria on contact. Only a tiny amount is needed. It will sting the nostrils if you use too much.

In addition to the Neti-Pot, I would use a Nebulizer sometimes with water and a little hydrogen peroxide. I breathed the vapor into my mouth and nasal passages. Again, this was to help kill any bacteria present in my sinuses or throat.

I also found that a daily intake of 1,000 to 2,000 mg of Vitamin B5 (Pantothenic acid) helped clear my sinuses. B5 supports the adrenal glands and helps reduce allergies. I received this tip from Dr. Frank Shallenberger[1] in his alternative health newsletter. He said to take 500-2500 mg of Vitamin B5 if you have allergies. I purchased the nutrient but didn't bother taking it. About two years later, I noticed that my wife struggled with stuffiness at night and regularly took an over-the-counter drug. I said you should try the B5. She took it and within 20 minutes, she had relief. I immediately tried it myself and also got relief. At this point, I consider it another miracle nutrient. We make sure we take our B5 with us when traveling.

After brushing, I decided to use a water pic on my teeth and gums to eliminate any remaining food particles that could aggravate the infection. Brushing my teeth daily and flossing as needed is essential. I did not want further complications to the infected root canal tooth, the bone loss, or the attached bridge via lousy hygiene.

Taking dental hygiene serious allows the nutrients the best effectiveness. I do not take any prescription drugs, nor had I taken any prescribed antibiotics for this particular bacteria infection. Based on my self-care alternative health protocols, I expected the root canal and bone infection to be healed or not healed.

As a contingency, I would take action to engage my dentist's solution if things got worse. This would be if intolerable pain started up, the tooth became obviously loose, or it was evident that the situation was getting worse and not better. That might include some inkling that the bone infection was spreading in my skull.

Anti-Inflammation Nutrients

I have developed an anti-inflammation protocol that I use. It also helps to alleviate pain in the body. These are the nutrients I use:

2 - Mega EFA (Essential Fatty Acids)

2 - Turmeric (Curcumin)

2 - Borage Oil (Gamma Linoleic Acid)

I purchase these nutrients from Vitacost.com and will use the nutrients twice a day if I am in trouble. That means six pills twice a day. I have used this protocol for tooth extractions and general pain relief without other pain medicines. The nutrients are natural pain killers; you can find them by searching Vitacost on the above names.

If you need additional pain relief, these nutraceuticals are also known for relieving pain.

Pain Relief Nutrients

◆ White Willow Bark Extract
◆ Boswellia (Indian Frankincense)
◆ Vitamin B6
◆ St John's Wort (Nerves)
◆ Alpha Lipoic Acid (Nerves)
◆ Serrapeptase

These are all pain relief ingredients available to you. The Pharma drug aspirin was created based on nature's White Willow Bark Extract, a natural salicin supplement. Frankincense was one of the three substances the Wise Men gifted to the baby Jesus.

Vitamin B6 is also a diuretic and can be overdone. If you experience tingling in the hands or feet, you are taking too much B6. St John's Wort is a mood-altering herb. One alternative doctor reported it as a little-known ingredient that helps heal nerves. Note: St John's Wort and other nutrients may interfere with prescribed medications. Check with your doctor or pharmacist for drug and nutrient conflicts.

Alpha Lipoic Acid is the number one nutrient to deal with nerve problems, according to YouTube's *Motivationaldoc*. Serrapeptase is also a little-known pain management ingredient developed from silk worms that helps to dissolve proteins, dissolve blood clots, and is known to reduce scars on the body.

Bone Support Nutrients

◆ Vitamin D3*
◆ Vitamin B6
◆ Vitamin K2*
◆ Calcium*
◆ Magnesium*
◆ Collagen*
◆ Vitamin C
◆ Silicon
◆ Copper
◆ Boron
◆ Zinc
◆ Manganese

There is a synergy between the ingredients marked with an asterisk*. Magnesium promotes calcium absorption in the intestines and helps activate calcium.

Calcium depends on Vitamin D for bone formation. Vitamin K2 helps cement calcium into the bones. Collagen has been reported to be at least 70% of the bone structure.

<u>Selecting Nutrients?</u>
<u>Don't Know Where To Start?</u>

Suppose you have a severe illness or disease and wonder how to find nutrients to help your body heal? If this is you, I recommend visiting Dr. Julian Whitaker's website at www.healthydirections.com. You will find several alternative medical experts with an incredible catalog of nutraceutical products that deal with various health issues.

Along with Dr. Whitaker, you will find cardiologist Dr. Stephen Sinatra and alternative Dr. David Williams, an expert in joint and digestion. At one time or another in the past, I had subscribed to all three of these alternative doctor newsletters. They are excellent doctors serving the alternative health care industry. Other doctors now work with them, including Dr. Stephen Sinatra's son, Dr. Drew Sinatra, a naturopathic doctor. This is a good starting point in your nutraceutical search for health solutions.

If you have diabetes, you will find a specific product already formulated to help you. Likewise, if you have heart problems, you will find Dr. Stephen Sinatra's heart product to help you. Finding a product already made for your health needs is an excellent start. Don't forget to take a good multivitamin. You will find some on the Healthy Directions website. The idea of a one-a-day multivitamin that literally paints the picture that you can take one pill daily and get the supplementation your body needs is fallacious. I take a men's multivitamin with six (6) capsules daily. The associated women's multivitamin has eight (8) pills a day. You cannot get what your body needs in a one-a-day formula. In addition, there is some evidence these types of multis simply pass through our system unabsorbed. A good multi is a necessary foundation for wellness and healing. I recommend a multi without iron unless your doctor says you need it. Most multis come in two versions, one without iron.

It has been over forty years since I subscribed to my first alternative health newsletter. It was Dr. Whitaker's. Soon after I subscribed, he sent me a note asking me about my most significant health challenge. I told him it was low back pain. He told me to take 1,000 mg of magnesium and six glasses of water a day. I took a multivitamin and had been supplementing with nutrients for years, so I thought I must be getting this already. To my surprise, I was only getting 10 mg of magnesium. I took his advice, and my low back pain just disappeared. I have told this to many people, and they have all eliminated their back pain. As it turns out, 70-90% of adults are deficient in magnesium. This nutrient is used in over 300 body functions. I supplement with magnesium because my multivitamin doesn't have enough to meet my needs. I take it about an hour before bedtime.

Whitaker's recommendation probably assumed magnesium oxide. It worked, but this version of magnesium has poor adsorption. A better product would be magnesium glycinate or L-Threonate (best absorption and for crossing the brain-blood barrier). I have found that taking 200 mg twice a day and adding more if needed works for me. If I experience loose stools, it means I am taking too much.

As an aside note, if I suffer from constipation, I simply take magnesium or Vitamin C. I increase my dosage until I resolve the constipation issue. At some point, I will resolve the issue. There is no need to take prescription drugs for this health issue. You may also consider adding essential fatty acids (EFA) or fish oils to your diet to alleviate constipation. Today, our bodies are exposed to too many Omega 6 oils from vegetable seed fats in the form of linoleic acid. Our body needs more Omega 3 oils (EFAs).

Dr. Whitaker makes an excellent eye product called

"Vision Gold Essentials." I wore glasses until age 60 when this product allowed me to ditch them. At age 76, I still do not wear glasses. If you have vision issues, this is a product you might want to check out. My eye doctor told me at age 40 that I needed bifocals. I never used the pair issued for me. At age 76, I still don't need them.

I can still read small print well, especially with good lighting. However, the image on many products is now getting smaller using 4-7 font sizes. Too much information is being crammed into limited space. The offset is shrinking the font size. As a result, I find reading glasses useful, especially in dim locations. I find the flashlight feature on my iPhone useful to see restaurant menus in dark lighting. This is probably my own fault at the moment. I simply have not been faithful with taking the eye nutrients I know I need.

I can confidently say this since I have had a strategy to take the eye nutrients and stop them when my vision is excellent. At some point, I encounter trouble reading small text. When I restart, the problem usually disappears in a couple of weeks. At 76, it would be better if I just took the nutrients daily. I like having good vision at an old age.

Now let's get back to the root canal and bone infection.

I believed I was experiencing healing. That meant I thought the bacterial infection was dying off. I believed my upper jaw bone was regrowing to fully support the tooth and its attached bridge.

How did I believe I was getting better? That is a good question; the answer lies in tuning into the body.

Eight months ago, I woke up and found 3-4 teeth on my mouth's upper right side were numb. It was like I had received a Novocain shot. That was when I contacted my dentist for an appointment. It took over two months for me to get in to see her. X-rays were taken on the root canal tooth when I explained why I wanted the check-up. The tooth did turn out to be a goner. The story continues in the "Health crisis parts 2 and 3." Unfortunately, my health had an unexpected and severe event that forced me to reevaluate and change my healing strategies.

———

The Health Crisis 2

The Subconscious Mind
Can Relive A Past Trauma Event

According to the "alternative doctor" Keith Scott-Mumby[1], "there are just four ways to conquer cancer:

1. Diet and nutrition

2. Chemical clean-up

3. Oxygen

4. Emotional unburdening."

Items two and four are the chemical and emotional detoxing of the body. Chemical clean-up of the body means eliminating external chemical influences affecting the body. You live across the street from a toxic chemical dump, etc. or toxic metals currently reside within your body. Emotionally unburdening the body means coming to grips and dealing with any past trauma your body has experienced. Why? Trauma buried inside us and ignored can eat away our physical bodies and well-being and lead to various diseases, not just cancer.

According to author Neville Goddard in his 1944 book, "Emotional disturbances, especially suppressed emotions, are the causes of all disease[2]." Medical science has confirmed that suppressed trauma can be a part of what is killing your body. How one deals with trauma is simple. You talk it out with someone who will listen.

Goddard's revelation on disease caused by emotional trauma in his 1944 book is not the only mid-20th Century health expose. G. Edward Griffin, 1952, wrote "A World Without Cancer[3] - The Story Of Vitamin B17." His cancer-cure discovery was a nutrient deficiency in the human body. Additional details are on a cancer website called informcentral.org. You will discover Dr. Johanna Budwig's cancer cure and other methods to approaching healing from an alternative health perspective. This suppressed cancer information is also 70+ years old. My first wife died of pancreatic cancer, and the impact of that trauma is relevant to this discussion.

You will find negative health information concerning alternative cancer cures online. Be aware that Big Pharma does not want you to cure cancer with simple methods like Dr. Griffin and Dr. Budwig. Both of their stories and cures are compelling and should be taken seriously. Web sites that disparage such simple health cures have an agenda in play. These anti-alternative health sites are financed by powerful interest groups like Big Pharma.

In December, I experienced tooth numbness and made a dental appointment for the following February 14th, Valentine's Day. That was when I was told the root canal tooth was a goner and that my jaw bone infection was serious. I discounted the dentist's characterization of the bone infection as *just* the dentist's perspective. I had a spiritual perspective to take into consideration. For me, that means there can be a different physical outcome. Yet, I do not have a dentist's education. I suppose this is where the physical and spiritual domains for healing can clash. I know they are not even in many minds. I might lean 70/30 or 60/40 in favor of the spiritual.

During the dental work, my systolic blood pressure was reading 165. I ignored this as an anomaly or white coat syndrome. Ignoring my blood pressure in February, and discounting the infection's serious characterization, would come back to haunt me as bad decisions. I'd been monitoring my blood pressure for decades, which typically measures around 124/84. I failed to realize that the jawbone infection was spreading, increasing my blood pressure.

It was now June 3rd, eight months after my journey with this health crisis began. I reminded myself to send my grandson Benjamin well wishes on his 25th birthday. Exactly 19 years ago, his grandmother Jackie died on his sixth birthday. The day before in 2003, my wife had told me she would pass the next day, which was Benjamin's birthday, and asked me what my plans were.

I told her we would have a birthday party for Benjamin's sixth birthday and celebrate his grandma Jackie getting her heavenly wings. I have new tears just having to think about this traumatic event, even though I know I have already dealt emotionally with this trauma. I believe I was trying to convey to my six-year-old grandson the comforting words of Jesus in John 14:28.

Jesus said: "If you loved me, you would rejoice because I said, 'I am going [back] to the Father [our God] ...'"

Jackie and I had a love affair that stretched 43 years. She was my high school sweetheart; we were married 10 days short of 39 years. Of course, grandson Benjamin was traumatized. He expressed his trauma to me in his late teens or early twenties as his other grandfather almost passed away on his birthday. I imagine that losing two grandparents on your birthday might cause emotional trauma and physical health consequences. Apparently, my "grandma got her heavenly wings" pitch didn't really assuage Benjamin's emotions 19 years ago.

When Jackie and I got the news of her inoperable pancreatic cancer, she thought she might have to call an ambulance for me. My body reacted in what felt like an elephant sitting on my chest. I had intense chest pain and trouble breathing. She thought I had a heart attack. I said no: "My heart is just broken." I could feel my heart being chopped apart as the spiritual bonds that held our love together were getting unwound. I knew it was her time.

At 2:30 am the day before the 19th anniversary of Jackie's passing, I went to bed with peace of mind and body. I was mindful that I wanted to wish Benjamin a happy 25th birthday. Undoubtedly, his grandma's passing still haunts the day for him and everyone else in the family.

Jackie and I had a similar event happen early in life. Our first son Glenn died five weeks after he was born. Unfortunately for the family, he died on Jackie's father Archie's birthday. Coincidently, it also happened to be the date of Jackie's parent's wedding anniversary. Try consciously or subconsciously avoiding that date every year with all the power of your mind!

Everyone deals with the death of a loved one in their own way. It's easy to move on for some and hard for others. Still, every year, a nagging feeling can arise around the date a loved one dies. Boom, a sad feeling sets in, and you don't really understand what's going on. Eventually, you realize, "Oh, it's that time of the year when so and so passed away." I witnessed Jackie experiencing this reality for decades. I also noticed my youngest daughter expressing the same unwanted mental and emotional intrusion around the date she lost her second son.

After I went to bed, I slept for a couple of hours and then awoke. I usually sleep in cycles, and waking after a couple of hours is routine. This time, however, was different as I had intense chest pain, back pain, indigestion, and some breathing difficulty. I took some Mylanta for gas and indigestion, which did not help. I drank a lot of water, which also did not help. I then used a moisturized hot pack to lay on. This gave me some relief.

I figured at the time that my nighttime nutrient intake of four grams of vitamin C might have created some issue. Many men might take this chest pain as a heart attack and rush to the emergency room. However, I can remember an experience similar to this one from my past. So, I was not concerned. I also thought that my heart was in good condition for a 76-year-old.

I returned to sleep and got up around 11:45 am. I noticed pain still in my chest. As I reflected on this death anniversary, I realized that my subconscious mind had caused me to relive physical pain. It was the pain I felt when Jackie received her doctor's death diagnosis. At that time, I took four kava pills to ease the anxiety from the subconscious-caused chest pain I was experiencing. I found myself reliving this past event and had to retake four kava pills to deal with the fear, stress, and pain.

I've known for a long time that the memories stored in our subconscious mind carry all the emotions we felt at the time with them. Want to re-experience the horror of a prior trauma? Just mentally think and reflect on such memories for a moment. Yes, if you drag up past trauma, you can relive it.

In my mind and perspective, I had dealt successfully with this trauma with many tears a long time ago. I lost my father at age 13 and my mother at age 21. Many other family members have passed, and I've also had to deal with their loss. When my dad died, my mother told me, "big boys don't cry!"

Without realizing it, my German mother was creating trauma for me, which I would later have to deal with on my own. I never had the chance to grieve the loss, say goodbye to my father, and shed my tears because of my mother's stoic culture. At age 21, aboard the USS Berkeley DDG-15, a guided-missile destroyer at sea duty off of Vietnam, I sat down to grieve with a good cry and tears over the loss of my father.

If losing my dad at age 13 wasn't enough trauma, my paternal grandparents in their mid-90s just disappeared. I was told they died when my father died, but I was not allowed to say goodbye or attend their funerals. For years, my father and I walked one and a half miles to his parent's home in North Minneapolis. We mowed their lawn, and in the winter, we shoveled their sidewalks. I remember my grandfather walking me at age five to the nearby Theodore Wirth Park and Glenwood Lake in the summer. From this perspective, I knew my paternal grandparents and how they loved me. For seven years during my youth, I was able to help my father with the chores my grandparents needed to have done. Then ... suddenly, they're just gone! To this day, I don't know when they died or what happened to them. Eventually, I will.

Death creates trauma, and the tears we shed over losing a loved one help us deal with death emotionally and not bury the trauma in our subconscious minds. I had never before experienced my subconscious mind creating physical body pain or health issues from a resurrected memory.

Science tells us we operate during the day, with 90% of our activities driven by the programming in our subconscious mind and its established habits. Only 10% of our day's activity is caused by the conscious choices of our mind. I suppose this is how "buried trauma" rears its ugly head and affects the health of our bodies.

Buried emotional trauma can result in our bodies living

in the sympathetic nervous system. This is the "fight or flight" condition where the body is always on edge, anxious, or filled with anxiety or fear. In contrast, our bodies can also live in the "rest, digest, & restore" mode by residing in our parasympathetic nervous system. It is worth studying and learning about these two health realities. Healing is said to only exist when we live in parasympathetic mode.

Ironically, our mind is not the only controlling factor regarding our health. Our bodies have a say in what is going on. To this extent, I have experienced a mind-body separation several times. Usually, it is my mind telling me everything is okay, and my body telling me something different physically. I can believe mentally, for example, that I am truly living in the parasympathetic nervous system where healing of my sickness occurs. Yet, my body doesn't believe it because my subconscious is running a program. Or something is really sick in the body, like a spreading bone infection.

You must examine past traumatic events in your life if you need healing because of a doctor's death diagnosis. You may not be mentally aware, but your subconscious mind may negatively affect your health. This could be a buried emotional trauma you've never fully dealt with. This is especially true if you have suppressed bitterness, anger, or resentments. Ancient wisdom tells us:

"A merry heart does good [healing], like medicine, But a broken spirit dries the bones." Proverbs 17:22

Could the physical pain or disease you're dealing with be from a past trauma memory buried and not fully dealt with? Stored in your subconscious mind and resurrected, affecting your health negatively and even against your conscious mind's decisions? Triggered by some event in your subconscious mind? Maybe a friend or family member's birthday that had coincided with the date of the past trauma?

Unfortunately, that is what my body experienced. It was frightening, especially since it wasn't a conscious thought of mine that resulted in the attending physical pain. It was involuntary and against my conscious mind and willpower.

This event and its terrible chest pain resulted from my subconscious mind reliving a past trauma I had dealt with and chose to forget. To put it in the past! Yet, how do you forget a grandson's birthday? Of course, the true answer is spiritual in nature.

Living life gives us issues and traumas we were never meant to deal with mentally. This is especially true of childhood traumas we carry into adulthood. I do not know of anyone who hasn't had childhood traumas. That includes my own children and grandchildren. I know that, in adulthood, it's on us, as adults, to figure out how to deal with the past traumas. Healing occurs when we can learn to let go and forgive our past, especially when we learn to forgive ourselves.

You, like me, need a mental bucket called: "God, this one belongs to you!" A place where we can let go of past things, events, or trauma that bother us emotionally or are unresolvable. A place mentally where we can dump on God and let Him deal with whatever is in the bucket. A place to let our bodies and minds get some peace. I don't believe it takes much genius to figure out the earth is a troubling place offering us a lot of pain, suffering, and misery. True genius occurs when you can mentally move beyond it by engaging your spiritual wits. Again, it's ancient wisdom for answers.

"Trust in the Lord with all your heart. And lean not on your own understanding." Proverbs 3:5

"Peace I leave with you. My peace I give to you: not as the world gives you do I give to you. Let not your heart be troubled ..." John 14:27

Little did I realize that the relived trauma would cause my blood pressure to elevate a lot higher. It was another lesson in how the mind can think everything is okay and how the body can smack you down and say, "no, you are not okay!"

In another eight days, I would suffer a devastating complication to my health. This time, the health crisis would really get the attention of my family and me. I had to dramatically change course. I was forced to forget my initial natural healing thoughts. The family absolutely blew a more concerning health care gasket. The story continues in part 3.

———

The Health Crisis 3

Wherever You Go, There You Are!

A hard reality that many people will not personally acknowledge, is the fact that we always find ourselves at a point in life exactly where our choices have led us. We all have to recognize that we are responsible for our own decisions. Yes, family and friends can pressure us to make different life choices. Yet, a healthy person must assume full responsibility for their choices in life. So, "wherever you go, there you are" - represents the reality of our life's choices.

I accept the consequences of my health care choices. I always have. As you consider your current health diagnosis, can you identify ways you've aggravated or contributed to the current situation? Do you accept you are exactly where your life choices have led you? Do you believe it is now up to you to fix the problem? Or to live with it in the case of something that cannot be fixed?

Yes, we suffer the consequences of our bad decisions. In this regard, I am no different than anyone else.

I made two bad decisions that resulted in high blood

pressure. The first one was the decision to ignore the jaw bone bacteria infection that was caused by my root canal. While the loss of jaw bone was significant, it didn't concern me at the time. What should have worried me in February was the systolic reading of 165. If I had been thinking clearly, I should have started daily BP readings at home and worked on my blood pressure. I have monitored blood pressure on and off over the years. In fact, a couple of years ago, I thought I was getting higher blood pressure and researched natural solutions.

At that time, I put myself on olive leaf extract, celery seed extract, and bromelain. My blood pressure (BP) dropped back into the normal range within a few days, so I stopped this BP protocol I had discovered. You can find articles attesting to these nutrients as natural BP reducers. I'm not sure why doctors prescribe Pharma drugs when natural food ingredients do the job.

Caution: You should not take these supplements if the doctor has you on blood pressure medication. You will need to first consult with your doctor. These natural nutrients might lower your blood pressure too much and put you into a state of hypotension. There are other issues involved with low pressure that might concern your health. Frankly, if it were I, I would stop taking the Pharma meds and start taking the natural nutraceuticals, which have no side effects. I also understand that the doctor might not know about natural high blood pressure solutions, or the doctor may not be able to recommend them if he knows due to "standard medical practices." A doctor can lose his medical license for not following Big Pharma's established standardized medical protocols. Add to that reality that most doctors are not trained in using nutrients or nutraceuticals for health problems. Yet, even this strategy is complicated by who has to pay for the drugs and nutrients. If you have a medical insurance plan that results in free medications, that might make the decision for you. With nutrients and nutraceuticals, you will have to pay the entire bill.

My wife went to a doctor recently to have her Covid-19 antibodies tested. They were robust even 14 months after we both contracted covid naturally. The doctor then measured her blood pressure at a whopping 180/120. Admittedly, she usually gets the "white coat syndrome," which elevates her blood pressure just by going to a doctor. Still, this was too high, so I immediately put her on the protocol I used. Her blood pressure has dropped below the recommended max resting rate of 120/80. Yet, I never checked my BP or returned to the BP protocol myself at that time.

High blood pressure is a silent killer. Usually, there are no physical symptoms present until some health issues arise. This can be a stroke, aneurism, heart attack, or another significant health event. So, while I chose to ignore the high blood pressure reading during my February 2022 dental appointment, it was a clue that I should not have overlooked. I was unaware that my BP was increasing to deal with an expanding and serious jaw bone infection. It was literally eating away at my upper jaw bone. When sick, your blood pressure can increase. That can happen when your body is sick, and in the case of my infection, I just wasn't thinking straight. Oops!

Now we arrive on June 11th. It was a beautiful sunny day in the Minneapolis area. My wife and I decided to go to Centennial Park near the Southdale shopping center in Edina. There, we planned to go paddle boating and play mini-golf. My wife had been there before, and I hadn't.

As I drove the car, I started feeling tired and sleepy. This is how I might feel driving at night during a long trip. However, this was in broad daylight, and I should have been wide awake. Admittedly, the previous night's sleep wasn't very good. Gradually, my vision started to become distorted. Initially, it started getting a little blurry, and then I saw double images of everything.

The car in front of me suddenly turned into two vehicles adjacent to each other in two visually separated lanes. Yikes. I quickly learned that if I closed one or the other eye, I would only see a single image. I wasn't sure exactly what was happening. My wife had to drive us home. I lost my confidence driving with the oddity of seeing two images. I was also unsure exactly what was going on and whether it might worsen, leading to other health problems. This occured on Saturday, June 11, 2022.

Of course, our thoughts immediately turned to the jaw bone infection and the unresolved root canal bacterial infection as the source. It seemed natural to blame the bone infection. This led to demands from the family to have the infected tooth removed before anything worse happened. After concerned calls to the dentist, the infected tooth was extracted on Monday, June 13, two days after the vision event.

The dental assistant tests blood pressure before any dental work is done. This time my BP was even higher and read 190/93. At a systolic level of 200, I was informed that no dental work would be done. I just barely squeezed under the wire to get the tooth extracted. This time the BP readings were getting my attention.

As an aside note, coffee can raise your blood pressure higher. As a much younger man seeking term life insurance of $250k, I had my first experience with too much coffee. I managed a group of field technicians and engineers servicing downtown Minneapolis's stock market and bank computers. I was consuming a pot of coffee each day.

On the date of my insurance exam, I was running late. I literally ran an estimated eight blocks to the insurance doctor's office. Of course, they slap an EKG machine on your body, and naturally, my heart wouldn't slow down to an acceptable level. I had to quit drinking coffee for two weeks and retake the exam. At that time, the doctor told me that the caffeine in one cup of coffee is used to jump-start a heart that stops. Unfortunately, I drank 3-4 cups of coffee daily, oblivious to my current and silently increasing blood pressure problem.

We talked to several health care professionals right after the vision event. They recommended I immediately go to an emergency room and get checked out. It turns out that there were two types of double vision. One type involves a single eye that has double vision issues. This is called monaural double vision. The second type is seeing double vision only when both eyes are open. Apparently, the second type, diplopia or binocular vision, is dangerous. It can involve a stroke, aneurism, or brain tumor.

The family went nuts when I had not removed the infected tooth, so, you don't have to wonder what happened when they discovered diplopia or double vision with both eyes open. I did not go to the emergency room to get checked out. Instead, my wife managed to get me into a local Ophthalmologist in two more days,

June 15. I had to wait an hour to see the first eye doctor. After testing, it appeared that my left eye could no longer pull to the left. Sometimes an eyeball doesn't track well due to an eye muscle, and an optical prism can be used to help the eye follow the image. In my case, the muscle that pulls the eyeball to the left was not working. My left eye would not move to the left of the center. Fortunately, a medical doctor specializing in double vision problems was available and saw me after the first eye specialist.

The double vision specialist ran several similar tests to the first doctor. Then, she ran some neurological tests on my head. All of these tests seemed normal, and no additional problems were noted. It appeared whatever happened affected only my left eye. We discussed issues, and I mentioned the high blood pressure Monday during the tooth extraction. This was only two days earlier, on June 13. She indicated that a BP of 190/93 could have caused the eye damage.

At the end of our meeting, the double vision expert wanted me to go to a hospital emergency room and get a brain MRI scan to rule out a more dangerous diagnosis, like an aneurism, tumor, or stroke. I rejected the brain scan as being an expensive test that wasn't needed. My reasoning was simple. I said: "If I play the devil's advocate, I can assume the worst-case scenario. Let's say there is a tumor or aneurism, or I had a stroke. If that were the case, I would not do anything about it. There won't be any brain surgery." I decided decades ago to forgo surgeries to extend my life. Instead, I decided to do my best to live the longest possible life. This is the faith I have. I suspect the horrible experiences my family has suffered at the hands of the allopathic medical establishment have reinforced this attitude. Still, it is where my faith is and helps explain why I won't invest in health insurance.

It goes beyond my faith, though, as money is involved. I spend around $300-400 a month on nutraceuticals. In this regard, I am investing in my body's health and longevity. It would cost at least that amount for medical insurance that provides no intrinsic value to my health unless I am a consumer of allopathic medical services, of which I am not. The unknown health reality is that allopathic medical services are very good at diagnostics and acute care. For example, if you broke an arm or were in an auto accident. However, they are very poor at chronic health problems such as cancer. This is my reality, so I focus on a nutraceutical approach to my health. If I break an arm, I will pay out of pocket. However, my car insurance will pay for the medical costs if I get into an auto accident. Will I regret this strategy?

Family members wanted me to get on a course of antibiotics to help deal with the jaw bone infection. My dentist prescribed me ten days on 800 mg of Amoxicillin. I do not use medical drugs but consented to antibiotic treatment to assuage the family. They were in dismay at the idea I would not get a brain scan. I realize that modern medicine can work miracles in many situations. I also recognize that modern medicine is the 3rd highest cause of death[1] in this country. Just after heart attacks and cancer, medical error caused deaths are estimated at 250,000 deaths annually in a John Hopkin's Study[2].

My grandparents lived into their mid-90s without any allopathic medical intervention. I plan to care for myself the best I can and live however long God wants me to live. Yes, there is a time to die. My faith tells me there is a place for me after I shed this human body. Scripture tells us that a good life is three score and ten, that is 70 years. Scripture also tells us a strong life is eighty years. In that regard at my current age of 76, I am on borrowed time.

Yet, I've always loved Genesis 6:3, where God says, "My Spirit shall not strive with man forever, for he is indeed flesh; yet his days shall be one hundred and twenty years." For many decades now, this has been my goal. To live a Genesis 6:3 life. That means taking care of my health the best I can and accepting the consequences of my decisions. Admittedly, I think I blew it with my choices surrounding the bone infection and the blood pressure.

Of course, most family members are horrified by this spiritual line of thinking and my beliefs concerning the limits I have placed on my body for medical intervention.

The Eye Area Damaged - Star

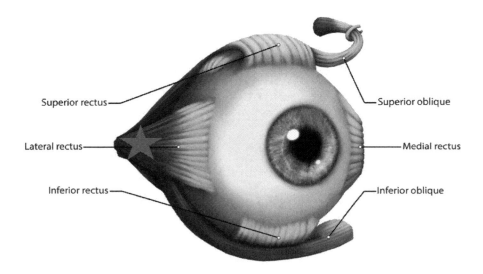

Superior rectus

Lateral rectus

Inferior rectus

Superior oblique

Medial rectus

Inferior oblique

Right eye

Double Vision Illustrated - The Left Eye (on right) Can't Move Left (to right) Like Right Eye (on left)

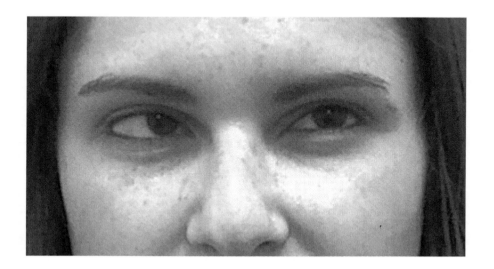

Summary Of Health Crisis

So, I started this health crisis with a jaw bone bacterial infection resulting from a root canal tooth gone awry. The bone of my upper jaw was getting eaten away by the bacterial infection. Unknowingly and by bad decisions on my part, my blood pressure was getting too high. Eventually, my high blood pressure blew a blood vessel dealing with the Lateral rectus in my left eye. It is probable a blood vessel that feeds the nerve that controls the Lateral rectus muscle of the eye. The result is my left eye would not move to the left of the center resulting in an unsynchronized second image overlapping the first image feeding my brain. This translates into a blurred vision or double vision with both eyes open.

The method of coping is to block off the image of one eye. Since the right eye has a full range of motion, I started patching my left eye so my brain could register and see a single image. When I wrote, the patch on my left eye blocked the second image in my brain. I also wore reading glasses and had the text enlarged on my computer screen for easy viewing.

I read at least four hours daily and when halfway through writing this book, everything ranged from blurred vision to seeing double images without patching an eye. I could see single images at times with both eyes. This occurred when my head was tilted left, and I looked toward the far right to see.

What was the prognosis? They told me there was a good chance my body would recover its sight in 6-12 weeks. What was the worse case? I suspected I'd have to live with the eye problem my remaining time on earth. However, I chose to believe I was being healed. That is what I programmed my subconscious mind with.

By July 11, 2022, I had reduced my blood pressure to 116/70 using the BP nutrients I identified earlier. On the 13th, I planned to see the eye specialist in double vision again. My wife was researching options for a low-cost brain MRI scan. I agreed to ask the doctor for a brain scan referral, assuming she still wanted one.

Many in the family were shocked that I hadn't had a brain scan yet. They believed that if they were me they would "need to know" what was going on. However, I have spent my life working in the electronics and computer fields, where weird things always happen. In many cases, something happens that baffles the mind and leaves you guessing as to what has just happened, and often without any ability to resolve the event.

If you always have to understand everything, you might go a little crazy. Having lived a life dealing with many ambiguities and unexplainable events in my life, I really don't need to know. I'm spiritually satisfied that God is in control. I don't need to be. He understands the things that happen even if I don't. The most outstanding education I have ever achieved in this life is the understanding that in the really big picture, I don't know that much. Just walk into any library and ponder what you think you might know. Then, be humble enough to admit there is a lot of knowledge in the world that we know very little about.

What's next? A conversation about my vision with the medical doctor who is a double-vision expert.

My wife believed my left eye was starting to move to

the left of its center. I could see a little movement, but for the most part, I was still seeing blurred or double images. If true, this meant my left eye had slowly begun the healing process. Remember, the body really wants to heal itself.

Many stem cell products promise to put new stem cells into your body. Stem cells can presumably become any type of cell the body needs. At present, I am using two stem cell products.

One product is Lifewave's X39 patch, a stem cell patch about the size of a quarter. It is placed on the spine just below the neck. This is the location of a significant energy meridian of the body. This technology is photo-optical in nature. Our bodies emit energy, which can be observed using modern technology.

The X39 patch reflects a specific frequency back into the body. The frequency reflected back into the body increases a copper peptide inside the body. This then results in an increase in brand new stem cells. The new stem cells are then used wherever the body needs them.

I've been using the X39 patch for the last 15 months and plan to continue using them for at least another year. I have experienced renewed body parts. There are several areas in which I know my body has seen improvements, but two items stick out in dramatic ways.

The first item is my spine. I injured my low back and

neck from prior accidents. Since the injuries and before using the stem cell patches, my neck and low back constantly shifted and moved. Both would quickly go out of place. Since using the X39 patch, both my low back and neck have become firm again and no longer move out of place so easily.

Another area of my back was also suffering a lot of mid-back pain. This, too, appears to be gone. I have no other way to explain how my low back, neck, and mid-back improved so much.

The other dramatic improvement occurred in my left hand. For over 18 years, I could not close my left hand and form a fist due to a trigger finger in my middle finger. This occurred in both hands simultaneously from overuse during a move in 2003. My right hand healed very fast in 1-2 years. My left hand never healed until after about 5 months of using the X39 patch[1]. I still have some issues, so I will keep using the product.

I just started using the second stem cell product after my eye event. This product is called "Active Stem[2]." It is a berry powder that is focused on creating new stem cells.

According to the product's website, "Active Stem is a cutting-edge blend of 5 powerful ingredients which, in clinical studies, have been shown to boost adult stem cell proliferation in vitro. If you are passionate about your health and want to maximize your potential, Active Stem is for you."

I cannot give you my impression of this particular product, but I plan on using it since I have it on hand. In any case, you need to be aware that many products are available that focus on increasing stem cells in your body. If stem cells do increase, it will help your body repair itself.

Another nutraceutical or alternative healing approach concerns the telomeres at the end of our chromosomes. Telomeres function like the ends of shoelaces, where a plastic cover keeps shoelaces from unraveling. Telomeres protect chromosomes and affect cellular division. As we age, the telomeres start to shorten. The shorter telomeres become, the shorter the remaining cellular life (division).

According to https://www.genome.gov/genetics-glossary/Telomere, "A telomere is a region of repetitive DNA sequences at the end of a chromosome. Telomeres protect the ends of chromosomes from becoming frayed or tangled. Each time a cell divides, the telomeres become slightly shorter. Eventually, they become so short that the cell can no longer divide successfully, and dies."

For many years now, I have taken many nutrients responsible for lengthening telomeres. Ingredients such as Turmeric can lengthen telomeres. You can research telomere nutrients or purchase a formulated product online. Yes, it's possible to grow younger as you age, but it will cost you time and money.

Well, back to my second appointment with the eye specialists. My daughter drove me over to the eye doctor. When the technician ran his eye tests, two improvements were noted. All the images presented the first time were seen in double by my vision. This time they were mostly single as I looked straight at the image. The second improvement was using prisms to see if my left eye could be moved into sync with the right eye. To my surprise, the prisms worked. This means my left eye had progressed enough to the left to eliminate double images when looking straight.

The eye doctor confirmed the slight improvement in my vision. She indicated no when asked whether she still thought I needed a brain scan. My blood pressure had been deemed the culprit, and she didn't think an MRI scan would reveal much. The bottom line was we will keep checking every month. At the end of six months, if the eye is not back to normal, the recommendation would be either surgery or the use of prism eyeglasses. I guess I can live with prism glasses if needed. She offered a loaner pair of glasses since the prism test was working. I declined since my eye would continue to move, and the prism would need changing. Instead, I continued blocking my left eye so I could see single images.

What can be learned from this and other health

experiences? That is the subject of chapter twelve.

———

CHAPTER FOUR
Whose Report Will You Believe?

TRUTH IS A SPIRITUAL CONSTRUCT

"Who has believed our report?" Isaiah 53:1

If I told you that truth is a "spiritual construct," what thoughts would run through your mind? Many people now believe they can have their own truth about a situation. If there are many people involved, can everyone have their own truth? Is there more than one truth about a given thing or situation? Or is there just one actual truth?

Consider some interesting images in which, if you look one way, you might see a witch, or in another, you can see a princess. There are many similar drawings. Some people will only see one of the two images present. However, the truth in this situation is that there are two images in the picture, not just one. Our eyes can play a lot of tricks. Still, the truth of this situation is that even though there are two images present, many people will never be able to see both of them. Therefore, some people will never know the actual truth of the drawing. However, this reality will not keep people from arguing about which image exists or whether two images do exist simultaneously.

It is often said, without a complete understanding, "And you shall know the truth, and the truth shall make you free!" This scripture is almost always taken out of its context to argue for someone's particular truth. Consider the actual scripture involved and its context.

[31] "Then Jesus said to those Jews who <u>believed Him</u>, "If you <u>abide in My word</u>, you are <u>My disciples</u> indeed. [32] **And you shall know the truth, and the truth shall make you free.**" John 8:31-32 NKJV

The truth statement is in bold. The following three spiritual conditions are underlined. They provide context for knowing the truth.

1. It pertains to people who believed in Jesus.
2. It pertains to people who abide in God's Word.
3. It was for actual disciples of Jesus.

It can be noted that truth involves more than just our five physical senses. Or our particular version of the truth compared to someone else's version. There is a spiritual component to the truth that many people don't know. It might explain why one person can only see a single image and others can see both. Who can see and understand the absolute truth of the matter?

The statement, "Who has believed our report?" gets down to the real issue, doesn't it? Who knows the truth? In the age of Covid 19, this question has risen to the top in everyone's mind. Who can we believe nowadays regarding the ultimate doctor's death diagnosis? A Covid-19 death unless you get vaccinated?

Is Covid-19 A Death Sentence?

Exactly what are the truths about Covid-19? Consider the following sixteen statements and mark each one either true or false as you believe them to be.

Sixteen Covid-19 Statements
Truths Or Lies?

1. Covid-19 is a death sentence.
2. Covid-19 vaccines are not experimental.
3. Covid-19 injections are the same as other vaccines.
4. Covid-19 injections do not modify our DNA.
5. Covid-19 injections are safe.
6. Covid-19 injections are effective.

7. Covid-19 injections are necessary for everyone.
8. Covid-19 is a pandemic of the unvaccinated.
9. Covid-19 forced injection mandates are legal.
10. Covid-19 jabs do not violate Nuremberg Codes.
11. Covid-19 lockdowns saved lives.
12. Covid-19 forced mask-wearing saved lives.
13. Covid-19 social 6 feet distancing saved lives.
14. Covid-19 infections were not preventable.
15. Wearing a mask stops the spread of Covid.
16. Vaccinated people do not spread Covid.

Depending upon your source of Covid-19 pandemic information, your opinions on the above 16 items will vary greatly. Which items are true? Which are false? No matter what you think, you probably would agree that half of the population disagrees with the other half on these statements.

We now live in an era of propaganda regarding our ability to discern medical truths. No matter what your opinions are on almost any subject, you can be confident the internet now abounds with your exact opposite view.

Suppose you use Google for searching healthcare or medical information. In that case, you must be aware that Google censors all alternative medical information. We used to be able to dialog and discuss subjects like Covid-19 and why the injections were healthy or not. It used to be okay to sit across the kitchen table and debate the pros and cons of any subject matter.

Never before has there been the exact same response from over 190 countries around the globe regarding a virus. The same detailed agenda of mandated injections, lockdowns, masks, and social distancing was implemented globally. Never before has an economy been shut down to deal with a flu-like virus, especially with an unapproved and experimental injection.

The politics of Covid-19 have become a very heated debate. Depending upon your belief, you will die if you don't get a covid shot and one or two boosters. Or, you will die earlier if you get the experimental injections. However, the real issue in this chapter revolves around your ability to discern the truth.

As you seek to resolve a doctor's death diagnosis, you will need the truth. Only in that way can you achieve healing. The choice begins with whether or not you will stick with the medical doctor's opinions, no matter what else you hear.

Reticular Activating System

Of course, and by now, you probably know that it is not as simple as just listening to your doctor or not. Our brains have what is referred to as the RAS or reticular activation system. It is part of our lizard brain that keeps our body breathing, heart pumping, etc.

However, the RAS is a gatekeeper for our brains. Based on our beliefs, it is where new information is allowed into our brains for consideration or rejection. Yes, our brains have a built-in confirmation bias. This means your brain automatically allows information you inherently agree with and rejects information you usually won't agree with.

Why is this? It's straightforward, a matter of survival. If your brain allowed in all the information it is exposed to, you couldn't survive very long. Therefore, the RAS is there to protect you from getting overwhelmed.

For example, you have now considered the sixteen items on the Covid-19 truth or lie list. Virtually all items on the list are false. If you don't realize this reality, you owe it to yourself to do some additional Covid-19 research from alternative doctors.

So the most challenging and first decision you will make will be whether or not you'll take the doctor's death diagnosis to heart. The second decision is how much it is worth to you to survive. Do you have a reason for continuing to live? What is it? The third decision is whether you will consider alternative healing strategies.

Yet, you have been programmed all of your life to believe and obey your medical doctor, haven't you? Isn't that why you will take your doctor's opinion over anyone involved in alternative health solutions? Now enters your very own built-in information filter. The RAS will work hard to help you reinforce your decision that it's best to stick with the doctor and his diagnosis.

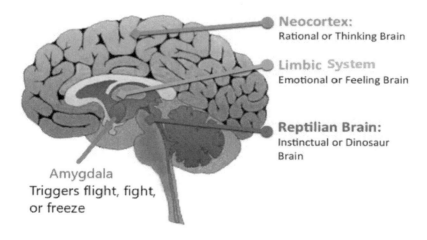

Neocortex:
Rational or Thinking Brain

Limbic System
Emotional or Feeling Brain

Reptilian Brain:
Instinctual or Dinosaur Brain

Amygdala
Triggers flight, fight, or freeze

The RAS is located in the brain stem near the top of your reptilian brain, aka "the lizard brain." This is shown in the following image. Note that the RAS influences the Neocortex, which is your rational and thinking brain.

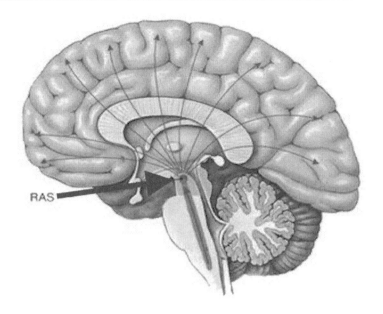

"Birds of a feather, flock together" is an ancient truism. Strangely, it does seem to reflect the reality of the brain's built-in RAS. Still, is all that we do just to agree with those who agree with us? If so, what does that say about our level of education? What about our ability to dialog with those who disagree with us?

Are you faced with a doctor's death diagnosis? Then, you'll need to think outside the box. In this sense, it means thinking outside the brain's RAS. You'll need to open up your mind to thoughts of possibilities outside the realm of what your brain thinks is true. You'll also have to broaden the ideas of what you believe is true. You will need healing truths to deal with a doctor's death diagnosis. To get them, think outside the realm of allopathic or standardized medical procedures. Engage your spiritual side for more healing truths. Because ...

__Truth Is A Spiritual Construct!__

CHAPTER FIVE
Covid-19 Health Protocols

THE POWER OF BELIEF

Germ Theory Vs Terrain Theory

Everyone in the United States has the right to expect only the truth from our government agencies. The CDC (Center for Disease Control), the NIH (National Institute of Health), the FDA (Food and Drug Administration), and every other agency involved in creating and approving a vaccine designed to help our bodies cope with a disease, and in making sure the food we eat is safe.

In the case of Covid-19, when they repeatedly stated that the vaccine is "safe and effective," you have the right to believe that such a statement is the absolute truth. Yet, when the government's own vaccine injury database[1] indicates that over 28,000 deaths have occurred from the vaccine, it's a good enough reason to question the integrity of the government.

When I was a married 18-year-old and my first wife was a 17-year-old, we were both smokers. We had heard that smoking while on birth control bills posed a danger of having a stroke. A close friend of ours actually had a stroke caused by smoking and being on birth control pills. When we questioned our doctor about the safety of birth control pills, he said, "This only happens to 1 in 300,000." Well, it happened to our 18-year-old friend. As a result, my wife and I decided to stop using birth control pills. The issue of safety involves "informed consent." Are you being informed of the dangers of medical treatments? Or are they being passed off as inconsequential by doctors? Are you asking about them?

It is the same with virtually all standardized medical care, along with every vaccine issued by Big Pharma. Do you have the right to believe the government and the medical establishment are telling you the truth? If so, then it includes the right to be fully informed about the possible dangers of the treatment, doesn't it?

My first wife was told she needed a CT scan for a health issue. They had her lay on her side on a gurney and injected dye into her neck vein. We were never told there was any danger. However, after the dye was injected, the nurse said, "Now, don't move. It could kill you!" What? I'll never forget how we both felt used by the medical staff. I'm not sure we would have consented to the procedure, but I am absolutely sure we would have liked to have been informed. You might ask, "if the procedure is safe, why do I sign an indemnity form before it starts?" If I didn't release the doctor and hospital from all liabilities, would they still perform the procedure on me? You might say we are trusting souls who "BELIEVE" we'll be okay.

So, from my perspective, if the Covid-19 vaccines were "safe and effective," there wouldn't be 28,000 deaths associated with the jab. I don't want to get into Covid-19 politics or the pros and cons of being vaccinated but be warned. The Covid-19 vaccinations are not what they are portrayed to be, and you take the jab at your own risk. Please do not vaccinate children. They are not at risk. If fact, 99% of the population is not at risk of getting seriously sick or dying from Covid-19. We should all expect colds or flu-like symptoms. Getting seriously ill or dying from Covid-19 mainly affected people over 60 and those with comorbidities. All this information is available online, as long as you don't search for it using Google.

My wife and I both had Covid-19 at Christmas in 2020. I was 74, and my symptoms began with some lethargy for five days. Then, I lost my sense of taste and smell for four-five days. After my body's senses returned, I experienced night sweats for about a week, waking to soaked bedsheets. For me, Covid-19 was a nuisance but nothing threatening to my life. It was because I had been feeding my immune system, feeding my body's terrain.

This gets me back to the first part of this chapter. It's about germ theory[2] vs. terrain theory[3]. I'll get to the Covid health protocols soon. The germ theory in medicine says that all disease is caused by some microbe, a virus, bacteria, or other microbes. To respond to the disease, we need to defend ourselves, and we do this with vaccines created by Big Pharma. The last time I checked, it looked like about 200 vaccines for adults might be in the pipeline. Big Pharma wants to vaccinate you for everything, and do so annually if they could.

I'll mention here that I am not a big fan of vaccines, even though with 7 1/2 years in Naval service, I think I was injected with everything the government had. But today's vaccines are not the same as those of the 60s. We now have media propaganda and government demands for annual flu vaccines for seniors and children. There is not a single study on the efficacy of yearly flu vaccines. Yet, many tactics scare people into getting annual flu shots. Like Covid-19, influenza is not something to be scared about unless you have a weak immune system.

The last flu vaccine I was associated with was when my first wife, who died of pancreatic cancer in 2003, wanted to get the flu shot about 23 years ago. I took her to the local grocery store, where they gave the flu injections for only $12. As she got the shot, I watched as she had an immediate anaphylactic reaction. She passed out, and an emergency crew gave her an epinephrine shot for her severe allergic reaction. The medics had to transport her to a hospital in an ambulance, where she spent four hours recovering. That $12 vaccine cost me over $1,000 between the ambulance ride, doctor, and emergency room costs. Vaccines can have side effects.

Childhood vaccination schedules are now a rightful concern for many parents. While Autism hasn't been proven to be conclusively caused by vaccines, the rates of Autism have a direct correlation to the increased schedule of childhood vaccinations. All vaccines have neurotoxins in them, which are passed off as innocent. Vaccines typically use aluminum as an adjuvant to aid in getting the immune system to react faster to the shot.

Aluminum is a known neurotoxin to the brain, and mercury, used in a product called Thimerosal, is still used in vaccines as a preservative. According to the CDC website, this is particularly true in multi-dose vaccine bottles. How do you know if your child's vaccine was from a multi-dose bottle? You can assume that as being true unless you ask your doctor. Do your children a favor. Demand single-dose vaccines without Thimerosal or other neurotoxins.

Autism was rare[4], and estimated to affect only 1 in

10,000 children in the 70s. Today, it is said to affect 1 in 50 children. It can be tied directly to the schedule of childhood vaccines. Childhood vaccines increased from around 6 in 1970 to over 70 for children under 18. Why do we inject all these vaccines into children? Why are there over 200 adult vaccines in the pipeline? It all gets back to the myth that microbes are the cause of all diseases. If microbes aren't the cause of disease, and we need to focus on our body's immunity, do we still need vaccines?

Vaccines are a pretty good profit tool when you think about it. Big Pharma gets to scare the dickens out of us with unseen microscopic creatures that can kill us. Then make big money jabbing us with vaccines. Even better, they get to do this without liability if something goes wrong. There are too many incidents of children getting harmed from vaccine injections to be so easily discounted. Children are getting Autism, and seniors are getting Alzheimer's. The sheer volume of the vaccine neurotoxins, like aluminum and mercury, injected into their bodies may cause these two diseases and others.

The Terrain Theory Contrast

In stark contrast to the germ theory of disease is the terrain theory of disease. In the terrain theory, microbes do not cause disease. In this theory, our bodies build disease from within, caused by weak immune systems. In other words, sickness is manifested inside unhealthy bodies and disease cannot occur in healthy bodies.

Healthy bodies, according to terrain theory, state that disease is caused by multiple factors. Like dehydration, malnutrition, toxicity, the environment, electromagnetic radiation, and even psychology (yes, our beliefs). It is up to us to keep our bodies healthy. If we do this, there is no need to fear microbes. Likewise, there is no need to live in fear.

Germ theory cannot explain why only some people will come down with viruses and others in the same crowd will not succumb. Terrain theory explains this reality because some people are healthy and others are not. Alternative healing thoughts on cancer state that a body in an alkaline state (healthy) cannot get cancer. Conversely, a body in an acidic state can quickly get cancer and other diseases.

I tested my first wife, who died of cancer. Her saliva read 5.5 or highly acidic on a pH strip. An acidic body is prone to sickness, and an acidic pH reading is typical for people with cancer. Mine read 7.1, which is alkaline and standard for healthy people. Ph strips are low-cost and are readily available for testing your saliva and blood. It is a good read on the overall health of your body. It is also a measuring stick to reversing cancer if you need one for periodic progress checks.

Now let's talk about the belief we hold in our minds and how those beliefs affect the health of our bodies.

Placebo, Nocebo, Faith & Belief

The "Placebo Effect." What is this other than the belief in the mind that the 'drug' being taken is working? Even though the patient has been given a sugar pill (placebo). In many instances, placebo results are strong and can have as much success as 50% when measured against real drug efficacies[5] in clinical drug trials. This gives rise to the issue of faith. Can a strong belief or faith result in healing? Does prayer affect healing? It is now well documented in studies that the answer to both questions is resounding yes! Belief, faith, and prayer can result in healing.

Your Beliefs Affect Your Healing

"A 2014 study led by Kaptchuk and published in *Science Translational Medicine* explored this by testing how people reacted to migraine pain medication. One group took a migraine drug labeled with the drug's name, another took a placebo labeled "placebo," and a third group took nothing. The researchers discovered that the placebo was 50% as effective as the real drug to reduce pain after a migraine attack. "[6]

In this instance, the people who took the sugar pill believed they were getting the medicine, which had a 50% efficacy rate compared to the actual drug. We assume that when the doctor prescribes a medication, it will work. "But in 2003, a senior executive with pharmaceutical company GlaxoSmithKline made headlines by admitting that more than 90 percent of drugs work only in 30 to 50 percent of people." Source[7]

So, if you believe you are being healed with a drug, even though you're getting a sugar pill, it can work 50% of the time. This is a problem for Big Pharma's drugs. Why take medicine if a drug is less effective than a placebo.

On the other end of belief is the issue of Nocebo. This is where people do not believe they are being healed. They do not think the medicine is working.

nocebo[8] nō-sē'bō noun

"A substance that causes undesirable side effects *as a result of a patient's perception that it is harmful* rather than as a result of a causative ingredient.

A substance which a patient experiences as harmful due to previous negative perception, but which is in fact pharmacologically (medicinally) inactive."

So, the mind works both ways. You can get a positive effect from a placebo (sugar pill) if you believe. Or, suppose you think the medicine is harmful. In that case, you can get negative health results, even if it is just a sugar pill.

If you have a doctor's death diagnosis, you must understand the power of your mind. I recommend you get a copy of the following two books to understand what healing means to your body. The first provides a new scientific understanding of how belief affects healing. It will explain why your brain can heal you and how the mind works. The second book gives you a sense of how robust the human body is from a regeneration point of view. Yes, the body constantly rebuilds itself, and it can rebuild healthier or not, depending on your inputs. Are you living a healthy or unhealthy lifestyle? Are you fostering good habits or still living with bad habits? If you had to change one habit now, what would you change? And if you changed the habit, would it improve your life?

Author Bruce H. Lipton in his excellent 2015 book, "The Biology Of Belief," explains what peace means to our human body from a biological perspective. When you spend this earthly journey living in peace, it facilitates healing in your physical body. In contrast, if you live in fear, it will promote disease and sickness. From a biological perspective, you must live this life in the parasympathetic nervous system as much as possible instead of the sympathetic nervous system. This is your body's mode for rest, digestion, and restoration. The latter is the fight or flight mode, which is based on fear.

[1] The parasympathetic nervous system is a subdivision of the autonomic nervous system. It is concerned with activities that generally inhibit or oppose the

physiological effects of the sympathetic nervous system.

[2] The sympathetic nervous system is the "fight or flight" part of the body that can speed up the heart and contract the blood vessels. It also regulates the function of glands, particularly the sweat glands. The sympathetic nervous system is activated under conditions of stress and fear.

So many people are committing suicide in today's world. I have to believe such behavior comes from a lack of mental peace. From my perspective, it doesn't take a genius to figure out that life on earth can be tormenting. Yet, all of this is spiritual to me. In a sermon by Norman Vincent Peale, he said, "How you expect to make it on this earth without the good God Almighty, I don't know." We are not built to carry the burdens of this life in our minds. We have to learn to live in the parasympathetic nervous system. There is no better way to understand this than with some ancient wisdom.

"YOU will keep him [or her] in perfect peace, whose mind is stayed on YOU because he [she] trusts in YOU[9]."

Isaiah 26:3

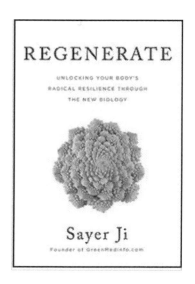

America now finds itself in massive censorship and a canceled culture regarding political matters. What is not so obvious is the censorship and control of information that affects your health and healing. If you only search Google, you will not find much information on health other than allopathic standardized medicine.

Doctors have trouble keeping up with developments in allopathic medicine. Are there any cures for cancer out there? Would you be surprised if I told you there were over 400 alternative approaches to healing cancer? Would you be surprised if I told you large doses of Vitamin C intravenously had been proven to cure cancer? Yet you will find such alternative healing information hard to locate. Google censors alternative healing data, as do social media sites like Facebook and Twitter. You'll need to use a different search engine like duckduckgo.com to find alternative health information. In this regard, you'll find that www.greenmedinfo.com is a valuable source for researching health information.

Sayer Ji, its founder, runs the site. He is also the author of *"Regenerate: Unlocking Your Body's Radical Resilience Through The New Biology."* Two essential health lessons found in *Regenerate* are:

"In our time, physicians have been indoctrinated and trained to match conditions with drugs and play symptom whack-a-mole, often making it impossible to discern patterns that have not already been stamped for approval by their peers." *Ji, Sayer. Regenerate (pp. 6-7). Hay House. Kindle Edition.*

"The New Biology unveils **three foundational facts about human health** that have highly empowering implications: DNA does not control your destiny. Epigenetic factors, or factors beyond the control of your genes (such as diet, lifestyle, environmental exposures, and mindset) almost exclusively determine your life-span and quality of life." *Ji, Sayer. Regenerate (p. 10).*

Regenerate is a complementary health education to the *"Biology of Belief"* by Bruce H. Lipton. These books also compliment my 2021 spiritual book, *"God And Healing,"* available at www.godandhealing.org.

If you take responsibility for your own health, these books are a good starting point in understanding what you are up against when it comes to healing. If you still have something to live for, you will have all the time you need to reverse the doctor's death diagnosis. That includes the body's ability to spontaneously heal and change a death trajectory.

Your Body Rebuilds Itself

"Within the next year, 95% of the cells in your body will die and be replaced. In 365 days, your body rebuilds[10] itself into something better (or worse), depending on how well you treat it."

Thinking about a knee, hip, or shoulder replacement? Someone asked me if I knew why Minnesota had so many hip replacement surgeries. When I asked why, I was told Minnesota had the highest number of orthopedic surgeons in the nation. Is this the reason so many joint replacements take place in Minnesota?

Your body can rebuild itself, and this reality extends to your knees, hips, and shoulders. It would be wise to try to feed your body's terrain what it needs first before deciding to replace a body part.

How The Body Rebuilds Itself

Body Part	Rebuild Time
Brain	1 Year
Blood	4 Months
Skin	1 Month
Lungs	2-3 Weeks
Bones	3 Months
DNA	2 Months
Liver	6 Weeks
Stomach	5 Days

Covid-19 Health Protocols

We're finally at the end of this chapter, where I will explain the health protocols for dealing with Covid-19 that I know. However, implementing a health protocol that feeds your terrain will cost you out of pocket. Your medical insurance plan will usually not pay for nutraceuticals. It might cost you well over $100 per month to feed your terrain what it needs to keep healthy.

At this point, you must face the difference between buying medical insurance and paying for products to keep you healthy. These are two separate health ideas. You buy medical insurance with a deductible and copay in the standard medical plan. Many people refuse to outlay money for things like a multivitamin. I've heard it said, "that's more than a copay if I get sick."

So, we're at a crossroads in healing. We are back to the germ theory vs. the terrain theory. All of these Covid-19 health protocols require the consumption of nutraceuticals and, by extension, money out of your pocket. I've already told you my strategy involves working on my body's terrain and not participating in the traditional approach to medical services. If you follow a Covid-19 health protocol, I recommend checking out vitacost.com. This is where I purchase almost all of the nutrients I take.

So, here we go. The first Covid-19 protocol is "A Guide to Home-Based Covid Treatment."

* * *

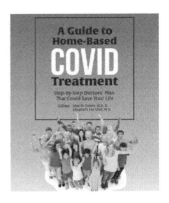

You can download this guide in PDF form from the *Association Of American Physicians and Surgeons* (AAPS) at https://aapsonline.org/covidpatientguide/.

An updated list of protocols in use for Covid early treatment and prevention can be found at https://c19protocols.com/.

<u>Dr. Richard Cheng MD, PhD</u>
Acute Covid-19 Protocols[11]

Used in the management of severe acute viral infections.
- ✓ Vitamin C - 10,000 mg/day in divided doses
    - Or IV Vitamin C
    - Or Liposomal Vitamin C - 2,000 mg 3-4x/day
- ✓ Vitamin D3 - 5,000 IU/day
    - Keep blood levels between 50-100 ng/ml.

- ✓ Vitamin E - 1,000 IU/day
- ✓ Liposomal Glutathione - 2,000 mg or more daily
  - Or Glutathione IV
- ✓ Magnesium - 500 to 1,000 mg/day
- ✓ Zinc - 50 to 100 mg/day for 7-10 days
- ✓ H202 Mouth wash/nasal rinse or nebulization
- ✓ Others:
  - Vitamin B complex
  - Other antioxidants
  - HCQ
  - Ivermectin

Disease Prevention Protocol
Dr. Brian Ardis[12]

Ardislabs.com

This protocol is used to keep your body healthy and can fight disease and even the Covid spike proteins remaining in the body.

- ✓ Vitamin C - 5,000 to 10,000 mg/day
  - In divided doses
- ✓ Vitamin D - 5,000 to 10,000 IU/day
- ✓ Selenium - 200 mcg/day
- ✓ Magnesium - 500 mg/day
- ✓ Apple Pectin - 700 mg/twice a day
- ✓ Zinc - 100 to 200 mg/day

✓   Vitamin K - 100 mg/day

Dr. Ardis' disease prevention protocol video.[13]

Notes:

- Use K2 and Magnesium with D3 and Zinc for best absorption.
- Apple Pectin binds to toxins in the body to eliminate them, which is expected to include the spike protein involved with covid.

If you want to heal your body or prevent the disease from quickly manifesting within your body, try using some of the nutrients in these health protocols.

CHAPTER SIX
Honesty, I Really Know Better!

"I can do all things through
Christ who strengthens me."
Philippians 4:13 (NKJV)

WHEN THE BODY SINGS, LISTEN

A large part of "Self Care" is learning to tune in and listen to what your body is trying to tell you. I will admit that this is an enormous challenge for me. Perhaps it is the biggest challenge when it comes to taking care of my own health needs. It's Tuesday, and last Sunday, I replaced a water valve for the cold water and filtered water to our kitchen sink. In the process, I became contorted and twisted under the sink in several ways. My back muscles were put out of shape and almost went spastic on me. Think of an impending Charlie horse on either side of your back, depending on which way you moved.

Last night as I tried to sleep, the right side of my back was in pain and ached. For the most part, I was successful in ignoring the pain. However, during the night, I got a hot pack and laid on that to get back to sleep.

My body was singing to me, but I wasn't listening. In fact, I was tuned out and should have known better. Over the years, I have increased my tolerance for pain, and I am sure that this is one of the reasons I could ignore the pain.

It was only the next morning that I realized I had not put any minerals into my body for 4-6 days. Specifically, magnesium, which is used in virtually all the muscles of the body. It is another way that I knew better, but at that moment, I did not remember. I now have decades of experience with how magnesium and other minerals impact my body. I even have a cheat sheet, where it is written down on how various nutrients are needed and why. This is to help me remember, but when I am "at the moment" — it is not something that readily comes to my mind.

I was tuned out. However, when your body sings to you, you need to tune in. It takes time and effort. I need to incorporate the cheat sheet I have on nutrient needs into a daily routine I can follow.

When your body has pain, it is trying to communicate with you. It is time to tune in to what is going on and mentally reflect on options you already know about. If you don't have a solution that readily comes to mind, you'll need to do some research. Alternatively, if your issue is severe, you need to go to a doctor for help.

You can create a diary of different body issues that come up and the solutions you've found. With this information, you can create a daily, weekly, and monthly routine to follow to improve your health.

Remember the old adage of "out of sight, out of mind." It's very accurate. Keep your nutrient needs front and center to avoid needless sufferings.

There are other nutrients besides magnesium that help with muscle-related health issues. My spastic back pain suffering was prolonged because I did not "tune in" to why I was in pain. I failed to consult a prior list I had created in which magnesium would have come to my mind. It's not the first time I have been "tuned out," and I suspect it won't be the last.

IMAGINATION VS WILL POWER

When we know what not to eat, but still do it — are we abusing our bodies? Did we learn a hard lesson about food earlier, but then forgot about it? Is food the actual lesson or just another contest of imagination vs. will power where our imagination wins? Maybe the real battle exists in our subconscious programming.

I recently ate a sandwich with lunchmeat loaded with nitrate preservatives. It was a case where my imagination overcame my will power. That night I suffered from pain throughout my body as it tried to cope with the nitrates. It was a poor choice, but the food always seems to taste good at the time.

I knew this wasn't a good choice because I have suffered before from eating processed meats that my body does not like. Ugh! It's like my imagination overcomes my ability to think straight, reason correctly, and even use some common sense.

The bottom line is that most of us have a list of things we know that we need to avoid. Yet, we often fall away from the memory of events and succumb to our imagination. Cakes are a classic illustration for me. They are always appealing to me. However, my body does not like something that is inside of cakes. If I eat a small piece of cake, within minutes, I will find myself with flatulence. I don't know what it is with cakes. I can eat cookies all day long and never have that experience. My body doesn't like cakes, processed meats, cow's milk, and other foods I am not even aware of.

Sometimes it is just habitual behavior like going to the movies and wanting popcorn, candy, and pop. I've done this for decades, yet this action now has consequences. I pay dearly with poor sleep and intestinal problems if I give in to my movie-going eating habits. Would it surprise you that I've known about this movie health issue for about three decades now? I still struggle with getting past the concession stand. It is now estimated that over 95% of all corn is GMO-based, which worsens the movie-going snack issue. Genetically modified corn, by my senses, literally smells terrible for the most part. I don't remember popcorn being that bad 4-5 decades ago.

Only God knows what the GMO products are doing to our health. We are in an era of Ag products that look beautiful and last forever but lack any significant nutritional value. Alternative doctors would say that the typical veggie and fruit product is no longer nutrient-dense. I know this reality, but the knowledge alone does not help my will power. Not when my imagination takes hold, as I get near the theatre's concession stand.

When we know what to do, but can't execute the correct behavior we want, it hurts our health. It is actually hurting our bodies, even though we'll all admit that we really know better.

What is it, you know that you need to do? Quit smoking? Quit drinking? Exercise? What keeps you from doing what you know you need to do? Is it your imagination?

For me? I think I get stubborn at times about food, or, at least, weak-willed. That is what consuming processed meats as an example means to me. Honestly, I really know better!

I DON'T RECALL? REALLY?

Our minds operate on both a conscious and a subconscious level. On a conscious level, you are mindful of your thoughts. You are acting with a purpose in whatever activity you are involved with. The conscious level of thinking is when your memory is actually engaged. You might as well say to yourself: "I am going to do this (name your activity) now." At that moment, your mind consciously creates a memory or mental marker of the activity.

In contrast, have you ever asked yourself whether you took a particular action, wondering if you really did? You might say to yourself, "I don't recall."

If that happens, odds are you have been operating on a subconscious level doing something routine. You are on autopilot and don't have to think on the conscious level with your mind. Now, if you were wondering if you had just brushed your teeth, the answer usually resolves itself fast. Often just running your tongue over your teeth will give you the answer. The lingering taste of the toothpaste may be another quick giveaway. Likewise, if you're wondering whether you had flushed the toilet, lifting the lid gives you a quick answer as will the noise of the tank refilling itself.

A similar experience happens when we are driving to a place we often go to. It doesn't matter if there is traffic or not. You can actually rely on your subconscious mind to get you to your destination while you are consciously thinking about another subject. Note: This is not the same as being distracted by your conscious mind while driving, which can be dangerous.

What's the point? You are not losing your mind or memory when you do routine things that do not require conscious thought. If you need to remember something, make a mental note of the activity or write it down in a journal.

HOW KNOWING BECOMES BELIEVING

How do we move from what might be "knowing" into action that is the result of "believing?" You can't get there without a conscious plan that includes a record of the events you need to get there. Where? To the new paradigm [1], you'd like to achieve.

This is how it has always been getting you from one goal to another. From elementary school to middle school, then through high school into a trade school. Alternatively to your Associate's Degree, Bachelor's

Degree, and then to a more advanced degree if college was your educational path.

A unique thing happens when your conscious mind *fully* defines a new paradigm for your life that you seek. Your subconscious mind will then take over, placing your goal (next standard for life) on autopilot. That is, of course, if you've moved from knowing to believing. In this instance, I'm talking about healing and a new level or standard of health despite a doctor's death diagnosis. This new standard concept applies to whenever you move to a higher level or new paradigm in your life, regardless of the subject.

The first step is to make it real and take it from a mental knowing or conscious mind level into believing where the subconscious mind can make it happen.

WHY YOU'LL NEED A ROUTINE

Your life, when viewed in its totality, could be thought of as the contents of a DVD video disc. The disc shows your life from birth to your current life situation and eventually to your death. Each stage in your life, or current position, could then be viewed as a paradigm. Your paradigm could be considered to be a groove on the disc that ironically keeps replaying itself over and over. It's like the Ground Hog Day movie, which continually repeats the same day over and over again. In your life's journey, your paradigm represents all of your habits. Combined with all other attributes of your life's history, it controls all of your actions and decisions.

If you're like me and historically have loved going to movies, this would include getting popcorn, candy, and pop from the concession stand. In fact, going to the movies without getting at least popcorn seems cruel to me.

Enter life and its aging challenges. You reach the early 30's and all of a sudden, your need for calories decreases. You don't make any reductions in food or drink intake, and guess what? Yes, all of a sudden, you are changing your belt size and bulging out all over the place. This is precisely when your imagination confronts your will power. It is also when your current paradigm [subconscious programming and habits that drive your daily activity] faces your conscious reasoning [thinking] ability. Note: Your subconscious mind doesn't think, it just acts on your behalf based on past programming from your life.

Your current situation or paradigm is what controls everything in your life. If you want to confront the health challenges you may be dealing with, you'll need to consider the paradigm of your life. What habits are part of your life? Good or bad? How is your current subconscious programming affecting your current activities and those actions you seek to change?

For five decades, I have wondered on and off about a single behavioral question. What it is that keeps people from acting on what they claim they believe? It's wondering why a fat doctor counsels weight loss to his diabetic patients but can't lose weight. It's wondering why a nurse who claims they know that smoking is terrible for their health but then sneaks out for smoke breaks throughout their workday. Why can't an alcoholic or drug addict change their behavior? It's not just the idea of addiction or, for that matter, even hypocrisy, albeit that might play a role. No, the real answer to my behavioral question is that our minds operate 95% of the day, thinking about various stuff. Actions usually take place without conscious efforts or thought. Our subconscious programming is what controls our activities throughout the day. Real change will only take place when we direct enough of our conscious thinking efforts long enough into laying down a new brain paradigm that, in essence, replaces the existing subconscious programming.

Therefore, confronting health issues like a doctor's death diagnosis means building new habits. It might mean creating a unique collection of practices that constitute a new paradigm for your life. It also means creating a routine to help you deal with whatever you need to do. If it is taking nutraceuticals to improve your health, those nutrients must be in-your-face so that you will be confronted with them daily. The saying: "Out of sight, out of mind" exists because it is a truism. If you place your multivitamin inside a cabinet, it is an absolute certainty that you will forget about it on some days of the week. Eventually, you might even forget about it entirely, unless you have reason to open the cabinet.

I would also add from my quality engineering work the phrase: "Don't expect what you do not inspect." This means journaling your progress by examining what is actually happening in your life regarding your health issues.

Using my movie concessions analogy or my processed meat nitrates health issue, I have come to a few conclusions. For one, I try to go to the movies when I am strong-willed. Note: This doesn't always work, but mentally I try to remind myself I will suffer later if I give in to my concession stand desires. Also, if I go with my wife, she helps me stay healthy. When it comes to processed meats, I have told her not to buy them anymore. We threw away the remaining two pounds of lunch meat that caused my suffering.

If you need to deal with a health issue, you *will* need to develop a new paradigm goal (new habits), and you will need a documented routine to help keep you on track. Think of this routine as a new set of practices and activities. These are daily actions you take and check off your list to get to the new health paradigm you want to be at. For example, you might have an item on your routine list to take 3,000 mg of Vitamin C daily to improve the health of your immune system.

HABITS & SUBCONSCIOUS MIND

The one huge question is this: "Are you operating with your subconscious mind in control?" Or, are you struggling with your conscious mind to accomplish what you need to do? Daily routines can eventually become habits. Once they are habits, you won't have to struggle to make things happen with your conscious mind. It means you are on autopilot with your healthcare needs and can skip the intentional effort steps.

Getting a task to operate on the subconscious level means you've developed a habit and no longer struggle with the issue on a conscious level. The angst of how-to, should-I, and all the other conscious level mental struggles trying to accomplish a goal is gone.

Get your new health or other habits on autopilot. Then you will have successfully created a new paradigm in life. This means you got out of the old rut and onto a new pathway in life. It means leaving your past life with its prior experience and starting again with new disciplines.

Shedding bad habits in favor of better health practices. Dropping an existing paradigm for your life to favor a new one to achieve something healthier and better for yourself. This means creating and learning to live with new daily health habits. It also means creating a healthier environment for your body to heal itself and stay fit.

"I can do all things through
Christ who strengthens me."
Philippians 4:13 (NKJV)

———

CHAPTER SEVEN
Focus On What You Can Control

Jesus said: "In this manner, therefore, pray: Our Father in heaven ..." Matthew 6:10 (NKJV)

WHAT YOU CAN'T CONTROL

There are many events during our earthly journey that are not within our ability to control or change. Circumstances that impact our lives in which, whether we like it or not, we are in the position of being an unwilling passenger on a ride we'd like to get off. These might include serious issues related to your health and the health of those whom you love. Some health issues, like a death diagnosis, are discussed in this book.

Take the 9/11 attacks or the more recent COVID-19 event. These are macro events that affect everyone's life. As of May 2020, an estimated 36-39 million people had lost their jobs in the coronavirus stay-at-home and shelter-in-place orders of Federal and State governments. Were you an essential worker, or did you lose your job like so many others? Did you have to wonder how to buy food or even pay your rent and utilities?

There are many things during our earthly journey that we have no control over. Think about simple things like sunshine and rain. Think about unexpected events. The truth is that many unknowns can impact our lives. For that reason, we can never really know 100% of what might happen next. These realities are ancient Scripture truths now largely forgotten by many.

"He [God] makes His sun rise on the evil and
on the good, and sends rain on the just and
on the unjust." Matthew 5:45 (NKJV) [1]

"When things are going well for you, be glad,
and when trouble comes, just remember: God sends
both happiness and trouble; you never know what
is going to happen next." Ecclesiastes 7:14 (TEV) [2]

Americans did not sign up or bargain to participate in the malaise of COVID-19. The coronavirus COVID-19 disease resulted in 75% of society becoming paralyzed with fear. Some were literally in fear of losing their lives. Families were not allowed to visit their elder members in long term care or senior facilities. Some older adults died alone without family members at their bedside to comfort them. It was not only scary, but it was also a disheartening time for everyone affected.

THE POWER OF PRAYER

I have a 96-year-old mother-in-law residing in a senior apartment in a small Minnesota town. The coronavirus threat to her bothers me to no end, and there is little associated with the situation that I can control. However, I can always send my prayers up to God for her protection. Yes, I am a spiritual man whose faith tells me that there is a God, and He listens to my prayers. When all else is lost, there is still the power of prayer. Praying is a spiritual choice that will always remain in everyone's ability to control. You can always make the spiritual choice using your thought processes to "Pray it up and play it [the crisis] down!" [3]

My mother-in-law has a strong faith in God and His Son Jesus. That fact is very comforting to me. However, I was not too fond of the fact she was confined. It's rare for a 96-year-old to be using modern technology devices. However, she uses a Windows 10 laptop, an iPhone 10x cell phone, a second older flip phone, and a VOIP home phone. She also accesses the internet off of a high-speed cable line using WiFi. All of this is quite interesting to me. I have been her tech support person, and when she needed help, she would FaceTime me. I could then guide her through technical issues as she pointed her iPhone camera to her laptop screen or other equipment.

Together, the family has found many ways within their control to help her. Some things still in the family's power, during the COVID-19 lockdown, were as follows:

- Technical support for her technology needs
- Shopping for her groceries & other essentials
- Bringing her prepared food
- Standing in the parking lot & talking on phones
- Running errands & dropping off supplies
- Meeting on opposite sides of a window
- Meeting outside 10 feet apart to speak in person

WHAT YOU CAN CONTROL

When you find yourself in a horrible situation, you'll have to do some creative thinking to determine what is actually within your ability to control. It's called "Possibility Thinking." [4]Start making a list of items you think are within your power to control. It's easy. Get a piece of paper and write down the numbers 1-20. Now start thinking about identifying the things within your ability to control. Keep writing until you identify twenty items. The first few items (1-7) will be easy for you to identify and list. The items further down the list (8-20) will require more creativity and brainpower. Still, they will be more useful to you during a crisis.

During the COVID-19 lockdown, some things you could still control might have included:

◆ Keeping in touch in person but at a distance
◆ Keeping in touch online using social media
◆ Calling and having a real phone conversation
◆ Meeting on FaceTime, Skype, or Zoom
◆ Reading a book
◆ Watching a good movie
◆ Taking some time to breathe, exercise, or meditate
◆ Taking some time to focus on nature
◆ Finding ways to thank people
◆ Finding ways to support people
◆ Eliminating a bad habit
◆ Creating a new habit
◆ Learning a new skill or trade
◆ Going back to school online - I.E., Udemy [5]

Why is creating a list of what you can control so important? Our mental and emotional health can be tied directly to how much we feel we control our lives. When we feel out of control, it is time to refocus on what we can still manage. Create a list geared to your life, and for the situation, you now find yourself in. You will be surprised at how much of your life is still within your ability to control. Even in a worldwide health crisis, there are many things still in your ability to control.

This exercise will help you mentally and emotionally detox from the stress that impacts your health. It works! I've personally been in several tough financial spots in my life. Creating a list of options is an excellent place to start. You can also create a second list by answering the following question. What can I do with my existing resources? It's the most critical question I've come to appreciate when I've been in a financial crisis. Every one of us has many resources. Often some of our resources are idle, ignored, not mentally recognized, or underused.

I'm not just talking about physical resources. You can also access spiritual, family, mental, and emotional mentors, along with other resources. You can bring these resources into your solutions list. For example, You can create a family or friend mastermind group and get more minds into your solutions list. Think outside the box and into the realm of "what's possible."

Another aspect of this creative exercise is to stay away from using the phrase "if only." For example, if only the bank would give me a loan, etc. Don't look for easy answers or the ones that pop quickly into your mind. Mentally dig deep for the creative solutions you'll need during a doctor's death diagnosis, other health crises, a financial crisis, or a personal crisis.

THE LAST HUMAN FREEDOM

The second item absolutely within your ability to control comes from Viktor Frankl's book: "Man's Search For Meaning." Viktor Frankl suffered at the hands of the Nazis in a concentration camp during World War II. During his time imprisoned, he watched many people suffer and die.

Everything was taken away from people; they were stripped naked and given little to eat to the point of starvation. Even under such dire circumstances, some people freely offered their food portions to other people suffering. Through this and other observations, Viktor Frankl observed that the last human freedom was the ability to choose your attitude and how you react to whatever is being done to you.

From my perspective, two items will always be within your power to control during this life. These two are your ability to pray to God and your ability to choose how you will respond to what is happening to you. You can quickly add to these two items by creating a list of things still under your control.

Be creative, and do a deep mind search. That is where you can find spiritual treasures and guidance from God. Yes, you may be in a very scary, sad, and profound health or financial crisis. But God and you are a majority.

It's an old spiritual statement that I found to be true after 76 years of life. With God's help, you can move forward, be healthier, achieve complete healing, be happier, and even more satisfied during your earthly journey.

A PRAYER PERSPECTIVE

From a spiritual perspective, we should live for God through our Lord Jesus Christ as the Apostle Paul taught in Holy Scripture. It means our prayers should be directed to the Father (Yahweh) in our Lord Jesus Christ's name. Praying to the Father is the truth of Holy Scripture despite Church teachings that you should pray to Jesus. Who you pray to is an important prayer and spiritual distinction that needs to be fully understood. Your prayers are yours to control. When you pray, follow the teachings of Christ and Apostle Paul.

"For even if there are so-called gods,
whether in heaven or on earth
(as there are many gods and many lords),
yet for us *there is* **one God, the Father,**
of whom *are* all things, and we for Him;
and one Lord Jesus Christ, through whom
are all things, and through whom we *live.*"
1 Corinthians 8:5-6 (NKJV)

Then Jesus said to him, "Away with
you, Satan! For it is written, 'You shall
worship the LORD your God, and Him
only you shall serve.' " Matthew 4:10 (NKJV)

[Jesus] said to them, "When you pray, say:
Our Father [God] in heaven, Hallowed be
Your [God's] name. Your [God's] kingdom come.
Your [God's] will be done ..." Luke 11:2 (NKJV)

"And in that day you will ask me [Jesus]
nothing. Most assuredly, I say to you,
whatever you ask the Father in my name
He [God] will give you." John 16:23 (NKJV)

Therefore, if you genuinely believe this Spiritual reality, you can understand that all things are possible through Christ Jesus, including healing. When we direct our prayers to God Himself in the name of His Son, our Lord Jesus Christ, we obey Scripture. When we pray to God, we honor the God that Jesus taught.

When we pray to God in our Lord Jesus Christ, we honor God's Son. It's not complicated, but you have to listen to God's Holy Word.

If you are a dedicated student of God's Word, it won't

take you long to realize how much the Orthodox Church teaches against it. Make your prayers more potent by sending them to God in Jesus' name.

"God is not a man ... Nor a son of man."
Numbers 23:19 (NKJV)

CHAPTER EIGHT
Don't Expect What You Don't Inspect

Vitamin C is such a powerful nutrient that it deserves a more detailed chapter explaining its many health benefits, protocols, and wonders. However, that's not my goal in this chapter. Instead, I will discuss Andrew W. Saul's Orthomolecular Medicine. Saul is widely known as "the Mega Vitamin Man." He has a lot of nutrient resources available on multiple websites. His website definition of orthomolecular medicine is as follows:

"Orthomolecular medicine describes the practice
of preventing and treating disease by providing the
body with optimal amounts of substances which
are natural to the body."

You will find detailed information on Vitamin C at this link. http://orthomolecular.org/nutrients/c.html

The rationale for intravenous Vitamin C therapy for cancer is located at this link. http://orthomolecular.org/library/ivccancerpt.shtml

Dr. Saul produced the "Vitamin Movie," which provides an overview of how vitamins (nutrients) can heal your body. It is available at this link.

https://dvd.thelivebettergroup.com/order-form1638140138637

Dr. Saul is also the author of the book "Doctor Yourself." It is an excellent resource and can be found at http://www.doctoryourself.com. There are free vitamin protocols on Saul's *doctor yourself* website. You'll find the following protocols -

◆ Riordan's IV Vitamin C

◆ How Vitamin C Repairs DNA

◆ Klenner's Multiple Sclerosis Protocol

◆ Shanghai Covid-19 Protocol

◆ Treating Tetanus with Vitamin C

You will also find nutrients listed in an A to Z list.

Article Archive A-Z:

Dr. Abram Hoffer:
The Final Interview

Absorption of Vit.C

Accidental Aerobics

Acid Reflux

ADHD / ADD

ADHD Book Review

AIDS

AIDS and Vitamin C

AIDS & Vitamins

Alcoholism

Alcoholism 2

Saul has written many books on the use of vitamins for healing. Some of the titles are as follows:

Andrew W. Saul, Ph.D., is an excellent resource for using vitamins to heal the body. Visit his many websites and explore some of his books.

Now, back to the discussion on tracking your progress on any goal. For illustration, I will use the tracking of my Vitamin C intake starting in the fall of 2020. After reading some of Saul's writings on Vitamin C, I decided to ramp up my Vitamin C intake to see its impact on my body. I had ramped up my intake for 4 1/2 months before contracting Covid-19 in December 2020. It may be why I felt my bout with Covid was not life threatening.

In late 2021, a friend got a severe case of Covid-19. Based on my studies, I rushed some Vitamin C powder over to him with instructions to ramp up at least 5 grams per hour or until he reached bowel tolerance. His doctor later told him it might have saved his life.

Exactly how much Vitamin C can you take? Saul suggests taking as much as you can until you reach bowel tolerance. This means until you have loose stools. Take too much, and you'll get diarrhea. You will need to back down your intake level if you reach this point.

One of the big lessons in taking nutraceuticals is that everyone's body is a little different and depends upon their body's terrain. My wife consumes lots of vegetables and fruits. I don't. Therefore, she cannot tolerate a lot of supplemental Vitamin C while I can. Our ability as an individual to handle different nutrients is tied directly to our body's terrain and its individual needs.

Track A Goal Using A Simple Run Chart

If you have a goal of any type, you'll need to track or chart your activity progress. Tracking and charting will help you reach your goals. Think of the weight loss and the monitoring of your weight, following the minutes of exercise per day, etc. Consuming vitamins in a specific quantity, like grams of Vitamin C daily, is no different. You won't document your progress if you don't track your daily intake. Having a visual chart is also motivating and helps you stay on track. If you have a paper graph or chart, you can quickly annotate the paper with notes explaining ups or downs, etc.

The simplest way to accomplish this is using graph paper and a pencil. You don't need anything more sophisticated. Keep it simple. Modern smartphones offer many other options like exercise, habit, and health trackers, making such goals easy to track.

Years ago, I purchased two books with blank graph paper that you can cut out and use with a copy machine. It's been a while, but I recently checked on Amazon to see if these easy chart and graphic paper books were still available. I found a used copy of the "Graphs & Charts" book online. A new edition of the "Graph Paper" book is also available. On Amazon, these books look like the two images below. The publisher and identification information is listed below the picture.

So my process for charting or graphing is pretty simple. I find a page with squares that looks like it covers the vertical and horizontal ranges I want, and then I copy it on my copier. Alternatively, it is also a simple matter to grab a piece of blank or lined paper and simply draw vertical and horizontal lines to record something. The emphasis here is on simplicity.

With modern computers, we've mostly forgotten how

simple it is to just use a piece of paper with a pencil to accomplish the task of recording and tracking something. You can contrast this simple activity with that of using a computer and software like Microsoft Excel. The key: Keep it simple! Make it easy for yourself to track your progress.

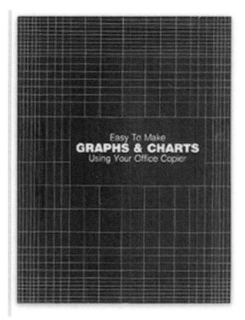

Publisher: Caddylak Systems, Inc.

ASIN: BOOAOUXW4

Publisher: Craver (Author)

ISBN-13: 978-1555610760

Don't Expect What You Don't Inspect!

I recommend a simple run chart with an X-Y axis, as shown below, to track the progress of any activity or habit you are working on. The four graphs shown next track my progress in ramping up my Vitamin C intake from August 2020 through January 2021. It covers the time when I contracted the Covid-19 virus.

Chart A Goal Into A Habit
Then Put It On Autopilot

Charting your progress will help to get your subconscious mind involved. This can get your task on autopilot fast. Getting on autopilot occurs when the task becomes a habit, and you no longer have to consciously think about it anymore.

I spent many years in manufacturing companies' quality control and engineering departments. Eventually, I held a job as Director of Quality for a $70 Million division of a significant manufacturer. From my experience in the quality engineering field comes the statement that is the title of this chapter. "Don't expect what you don't inspect!"

Keep vitamins in front of your face in your home or office, in a spot you can't ignore. Then track your daily intake on paper. You'll find that this "in your face" activity will aid in reaching your goals. It's not difficult, but it does take time and effort.

Here are my four Vitamin C intake graphs with descriptions and explanations of annotations (markups).

Vitamin C July-Sept 2020

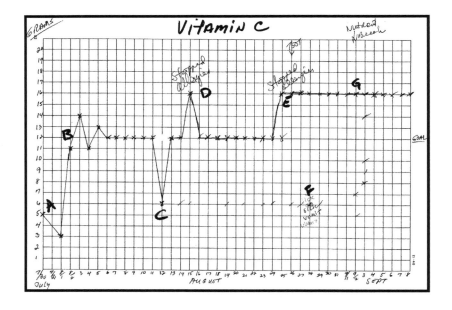

July-Sept Comments

Graph 1

- Graph starts on July 30, 2020
- Graph covers the entire month of August 2020
- Graph ends on September 8, 2020
- A-G characters are comments on the graph
- A - indicates the starting point of 5 grams/day
- B - indicates when I achieved 12 grams/day
- C - indicates a point where my intake was low
- D - indicates a point where my allergies stopped
- E - indicates I changed my goal to 16 grams/day
- F - indicates a day I was sick and vomited
- G - indicated I took a nutrient break (no intake)

As I was scaling up my Vitamin C intake, I noticed a distinct improvement in my allergies when I reached 16 grams. That encouraged me to ramp up to that level. It seemed my body could tolerate that level.

Vitamin C Sep-Oct 2020

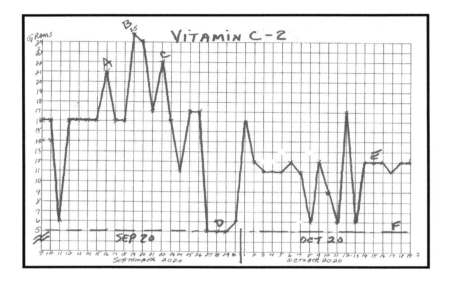

The most notable aspect of this chart are the ups and downs of my Vitamin C intake. Also, it's obvious, I was trying to see what 20-25 grams felt like. The primary reason for the fluctuations is that I was not following a written daily schedule. I was taking the nutrient as best I could remember during the day.

Sep-Oct Comments

Graph 2

- Graph starts on September 9, 2020
- Graph ends on October 19, 2020
- During most of September, I hit the 16 gram goal
- A - I achieved a 20 gram intake
- B - I peaked at 25 grams
- C - Illustrates my up and down intake levels
- D - I dropped down to a 5 gram intake level
- E - I got back up to a 12 gram/day intake level
- F - Is a line that shows the 5 gram chart line.

This illustrates to me that a schedule is required to be successful at such a daily routine. If it's not on your daily routine, it is not in habit form or driven by your mind's subconscious routines. In that case, it needs to be on a written schedule that is in your face daily. Alternatively, set up a series of reminders on your computer or smartphone.

Vitamin C Oct-Nov 2020

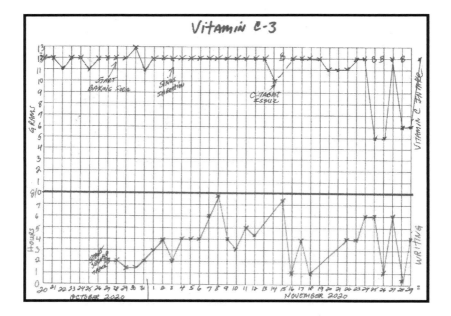

Oct-Nov Comments

<u>Graph 3</u>

- Graph starts on October 20, 2020
- Graph ends on November 29, 2020
- Graph has two levels, lower and upper
- Lower level tracks writing time in hours
- Upper level tracks Vitamin C intake
- Vitamin C intake relatively stable at 12 grams/day

When you create a graph to chart your progress, you can create two tracks on the same paper. In this case, I decided I wanted to track the hours in a day that I spent writing. This is the lower graph whose vertical scale is from 1-8 hours. The upper scale tracks Vitamin C intake and ranges from 0-13 grams/day. So, by this time, I've decided on the 12 grams daily goal.

Vitamin C Dec 2020-Jan 2021

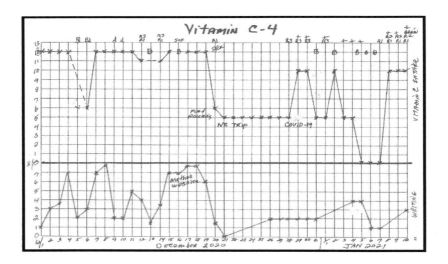

Dec-Jan Comments

<u>Graph 4</u>

- Graph starts December 1, 2020

- Graph ends January 10, 2021

- Graph covers entire month of December 2020

- At December 20, I dropped down to 5 grams/day

- At December 28, I caught Covid-19

- In late December-January, I am up and down again

- On January 4-6, I took no Vitamin C

Graph 4 illustrates again the difficulty of trying to maintain a nutrient goal. In this case, the goal is 12 grams/day. Again, the fluctuation is because I am not on a written schedule. There are some small letters at the top of the chart that refer to some other nutrient schedules I was experimenting with. This chart has the same scales as the prior chart. It too tracks the time I spent writing on the lower graph and Vitamin C on the upper graph.

CHAPTER NINE
Exploring The Health Sandbox

"But let each one examine his own
work, and then he will have
rejoicing in himself alone, and not
in another. For each one shall bear
his own load." Galatians 6:4-5 (NKJV)

Kids like playing in sandboxes. Without inhibitions or expectations, kids will jump in and start playing. There are no judgments, just a desire to play and explore. Children may lose confidence in their ability to play safely (in life) as they age. By adulthood, they may become programmed that only doctors have health answers.

Regarding nutraceuticals, there is another sandbox adults can play in and explore. It's your health sandbox! It is a sandbox of self-care options, alternative health approaches, and spiritual approaches to healing for your body. You start with little or no knowledge of how to play and explore, but then you learn as you go. You learn to play and experiment with your health as you play in your health sandbox. Early on, you might find a pre-formulated nutraceutical product for a current health problem. You might also seek out advisers (playmates) to help you.

Several alternative doctor newsletters may make various health statements about this or that nutrient helping a specific health condition. Exploring new information or experimenting with it is part of my health sandbox. Suppose whatever health condition they have is a solution that applies to me? In that case, I can either ignore the information or act on it. When I decide to take action, I order the nutrient and start consuming them. This is how I have acquired over 100 nutraceuticals in my sandbox (inventory). Suppose it is a nutrient or nutraceutical formulation that I think I need. In that case, I will order a 3-6 month supply because the body often needs some time for full efficacy.

I know from experience that it might take a while for nutrients to have their best effect on my body. If a nutrient is worth trying, it should be given 30-90 days to show you what it will do for your body. There are exceptions. Magnesium, for example, improved my low back pain within 72 hours. I believe Vitamin C needs a little time to build up in the body for best effectiveness.

Vitamin B5 works wonders on my allergies and sinuses

within 30 minutes. Yet our bodies depend on their own terrain, and we are all individuals with differing physical and nutrient needs. So, regarding a death diagnosis, remember there is a health sandbox with self-care, alternative, and spiritual healing options you can explore.

In the 70s, as a young man, it was my good fortune to read *"Passages: Predictable Crises Of Adult Life"* by Gail Sheehy (Paperback, January 1, 1977). Reading this book was like reading the history of my own life. The big shocker: our human life is not as unique as we'd like to think for most of us. We are all experiencing similar (sometimes identical) obstacles and crises during our adult journey on earth. It was like reading my future if I stayed in the direction Sheehy outlined in her book, and I didn't like that future. As a result, my wife and I decided to change the apparent course we were on.

We think we are unique and even one-of-a-kind as human beings. As a child of God, I believe that is true from a spiritual standpoint. We are individual spiritual beings. However, from a physical or body perspective, I think many of us face similar health problems or issues during this earthly journey. In that sense, we are not unique.

I believe our bodies face nutrient requirements at different levels and possibly in various combinations. We are indeed all playing in a health sandbox. Whether or not we realize it with our minds, our health sandbox is either healthy or filled with bad health habits. Still, ancient wisdom suggests that many things in this life are common to all humans.

"No temptation has overtaken you except such is common to man; but God is faithful, who will not allow you to be tempted beyond what you are able, but with the temptation will also make the way of escape, that you may be able to bear it." 1 Corinthians 10:13 NKJV

Disease and sicknesses related to bad habits are now confronting adults in their 40s and 50s. They include drinking, smoking, drugs, gambling, poor eating habits, or hygiene issues, etc. Those and other bad habits take little effort to get into but a lot of effort and energy to get out of or to change to something positive. Two of my cousins drank themselves to death in their mid-40s. One cousin died with the help of marijuana, further complicating their alcoholism. When a family member dies in their early to mid-40s, it is devastating to the family, especially children, siblings, nieces, and nephews.

If avoided in the 40s and 50s, deadly health habits will

often come roaring to life in the 60s and 70s. The solution is to be mindful of our health and habits at all ages. To live healthy throughout our adult lives. An informed adult realizes life is happier when good health is present. The old adage that "health is wealth" is absolutely true. Healthy adults also realize good health is something you must work at; it doesn't come without effort.

Precisely what is your eyesight worth? What about your hearing, sense of touch, sense of smell, arms, and legs? Would you sell off a kidney? When you think about the body and what it is capable of, most people won't put a price on a body part. Yes, health is wealth and having a healthy body is better than having an unhealthy body with a million dollars in the bank.

In my opinion, our adult lives don't just involve similar personal crises; they also involve similar or identical health issues and health crises. That doesn't mean you can't reach 100 years of age if you drink and smoke a lot. I'm sure everyone has heard about such lucky people and how even unlucky non-smokers develop lung cancer.

Still, there are some healthy things you can do in life and unhealthy things you can avoid. I also believe every person throughout their lives will have health issues. If not in their own body, then in the body of someone they love and care for, such as family and friends.

My first wife, Jackie, died from pancreatic cancer 98

days after her death diagnosis. Cancer is a silent killer, just like high blood pressure. Often there is little sign of anything serious until BAM! I've heard of many cases where someone is opened up for surgery only to find cancer raging throughout their body.

If you are dealing with a cancer diagnosis and don't know where to start, go to www.informcentral.org. You will find a cancer website with a lot of free information. When my wife got a doctor's death diagnosis, I researched cancer for weeks and read thousands of pages on alternative healing approaches. I've summarized them on this website and have a low-cost ($7.95) PDF eBook you can obtain at this site.

I learned a few lessons during our trip through this death diagnosis.

Hospice Lessons Learned

1) Take care of your health while you can.
2) If sick, you may not be able to care for yourself.
3) If deathly ill, you need a family member to help.

You will find help for your death diagnosis if you are in hospice care. That is, you will find compassionate people to help you die. Hospice workers may even resist any efforts to help you heal yourself. One of my friends had the hospice nurse take away her supply of nutrients. After all, it was time for her to die, wasn't it? Before entering hospice care, you must be within six months of death.

A hospice doctor stated that the average patient was on five-six prescribed drugs as they entered hospice. Of course, they weaned them off all their medications. Again, they were scheduled to die within six months, right? It has been reported[1] that, after 3 months off all the drugs, many hospice patients started to feel better[2] than they had in several years. What's that tell you about pharmaceutical drugs?

Remember when I said you needed a reason to live? Suppose you have a reason to keep living and still find yourself in hospice care, unable to care for yourself. In that case, you will need a family member to help you with a "stay alive plan." You may need help in consuming the nutraceuticals you need for healing. Vitamin C has been shown to heal cancer but takes large doses. A family member can help you follow the protocol I mentioned in the last chapter.

With pancreatic cancer, you may be unable to consume the necessary meds or nutrients. If you can't swallow pills or meds because they make you nauseous, you can take them anally. Larger empty capsules can be purchased online. You put the medications or smaller medications into larger empty pills and insert the larger capsules into the anus. They will then get absorbed into the body. Search the internet for the phrase "Home Vitamin Capsule Maker." You will find a variety of capsule sizes and how to make your own capsules.

What Would I Do?
I Would Focus On Oxygenating My Body

Suppose I had a cancer death diagnosis, what would I do? With what I know about health, I would deploy several anti-cancer protocols. But my focus would be on oxygenating my body. I would ramp up my Vitamin C intake to 50,000 to 100,000 mg daily. I assume I would not be able to get this done intravenously, so I would have to manage this intake in small doses every 15-60 minutes throughout the day. I would need some family help to achieve this level of intake. If you were in hospice, I expect they might also object to trying to heal yourself instead of just accepting your doctor's death diagnosis.

Vitamin C increases the level of hydrogen peroxide inside the body. This, in turn, increases the oxygen available to your cells. I would also use a nebulizer with

1% hydrogen peroxide.

It feels good when you walk on the beach barefoot, doesn't it? This is because when we are barefoot on the earth, our bodies are flooded with free electrons from the ground. This is referred to now as "grounding" or "earthing." There are many products available to help us with this healing technology. Therefore, I would also use grounding pads and bed sheets to allow maximum free electron intake from the earth into my body to repair electron-deficient cells. Search for "grounding pads" or "grounding bed sheets" for further information.

I would deploy apricot seeds following the protocol for using Vitamin B17. See informcentral.org for details.

I would also use Johanna Budwig's cancer cure using flax seed oil & cottage cheese. See informcentral.org.

Of course, I would throw everything but the kitchen sink at my body regarding nutraceuticals. Having said this, ramping up my Vitamin C intake by itself would be a full-time job. I'm sure I would need family help as well. This would be **my** preferred approach for any type of death diagnosis.

Hey, It's My Sandbox!

So, I would take advantage of my own sandbox and only

work with those medical professionals who will help me. They would allow for my opinions and offer informed consent on treatments. They would be a partner in my health decisions. They would not be a dictator of standard allopathic medical protocols.

If you have a doctor's death diagnosis, it probably came from an allopathic medical doctor. Therefore, the one thing I would recommend above all is to listen to your standard medical doctor. **But also** seek the help of a naturopath or functional medicine doctor. Preferably, this doctor would have experience with electroceutical techniques.

You'll need to explore options outside of standardized medical care. You'll need to think outside the box or you may be led to an early grave. Suppose the alternative doctor can analyze your body from an energy perspective. In that case, it will give you diagnostic insights your standard medical doctor doesn't even understand. They are usually ignorant of such technology and certainly not trained in it.

Following My Eye Event?

Seven weeks into the eye event of June 11, 2022, my left eye was beginning to heal, and I was able to write this page without seeing double or wearing an eye patch to block a double or blurred image. My left eye was healing, and I'm now expecting a full recovery. I may still have to engage in eye exercises to strengthen the left eye muscles. At this time, I no longer think I will need prism glasses. My blood pressure is measuring 116/75 at 69 pulses.

My body is regenerating as expected because I removed the cause of the eye damage. This was a bacteria-infected tooth eating away at my upper jaw and raising my blood pressure. The infected tooth (source) was removed, the jaw bone is being restored, and my blood pressure has returned to normal levels. Remove the cause of the disease or illness, feed the body what it needs, and it will regenerate health.

My Blood Pressure Protocol

I took my blood pressure of 190/93 down to normal almost immediately using Olive Leaf Extract, Celery Seed Extract, and Bromelain. This is what I took in terms of nutrients.

1) 1,000 mg of Olive Leaf Extract 2x/day
2) 1,000 mg of Celery Leaf Extract 2x/day
3) 833 mg of Bromelain at bedtime

* * *

If you search the internet (not using Google), you will find these nutrients all lower blood pressure naturally. If you visit a standard medical site, they will grudgingly admit they lower blood pressure but may try to obfuscate this reality. A note of caution is due here. If you are on a doctor's blood pressure med, seek their consultation before using these nutrients. If they are used with blood pressure meds, they may put you into hypotension. They could lower your blood pressure too much, which could cause other health problems.

This raises a natural question. Why are Big-Pharma drugs being prescribed frequently if such low-cost nutrients lower blood pressure? According to allopathic medicine, the current maximum blood pressure recommendation is 120/80. That means half of the adult population now has high blood pressure, and they qualify for Big Pharma's blood pressure drugs. For the last seven decades, max blood pressure has been recognized as 140/90. Why the change? I seriously don't believe half of the adult population is suddenly hypertensive. Because of the changes in what allopathic medicine now defines as the new and correct healthy systolic/diastolic numbers, medicine is recommended to more people more frequently. Can you say: "Follow the money?"

What About ALS?

A friend's ALS motivated me to write this book. So, what do I say about ALS? First, I would go for the oxygenation of the body as mentioned. Then, since we are in a sandbox, I would explore the internet for ALS cures.

When I typed "ALS cures" into the duckduckgo.com search engine, the top page was populated with allopathic medicine sites. Towards the bottom of the first page, I found "5 Natural Ways To Cure ALS". https://naturalnewsblogs.com/5-natural-ways-help-cure-als/.

The five natural ways to cure ALS are defined as follows:

1) Detox the body

2) Eat Organic

3) Avoid Sugar

4) Eat Coconut Oil

5) Self-Love and Forgiveness

All five recommendations are excellent from an alternative health and nutraceutical perspective. I gave my friend this health search strategy three years ago. I'm not sure about the progression of her ALS. I am sure this website along with the HealingALS[1] website has healing information for those diagnosed with ALS.

There is a wealth of information on how to deal with ALS. I fully expect this to be the case no matter what death sentence you've been given or what the death diagnosis is based upon. However, you will need to pay with the cost of your time to resolve your health issue, or perhaps someone in the family will assist you in your health research.

Item number five above is absolutely critical for the detoxing of our emotions. Any suppressed hatred, resentment, or bitterness are destructive to the human body for reasons I've already discussed.

There Is No Need To Fear
A Death Diagnosis

You Have A Health Sandbox

CHAPTER TEN
Self-Care Observations

"Behold, I am the Lord, the God of all flesh. Is there anything too hard for Me?" Jeremiah 32:27 NKJV

I am a man of faith, and I've often suspected that I made some deal with God. I did this as a kindergarten child in the Ascension Catholic School in North Minneapolis on Dupont Avenue at age 5. Why do I think that?

A few nights ago, I dreamed and remembered about placing a lit candle on a plastic kid's dinner plate under a mattress at our Minneapolis quadplex apartment on Dupont avenue. The bed started on fire. My dad saved the day by throwing the burning mattress over our second-story apartment railing. I think it burned itself out in the backyard of our apartment building.

In my dream, I found myself singing, "this little light of mine, I'm going to let it shine." Then it dawned on me, "Why would a child put a burning candle on a plate under a mattress?" Of course, it was to let my "light shine" in a place of darkness (under the mattress).

So, at age 76, I finally realized it might be a Catholic Nun's influence that led me to set a mattress on fire at age 5. How else does it make sense? Who else could have taught me the song? It had to be the teachers or Nuns at Ascension Catholic School during elementary class.

Remember These Lyrics?

- This little light of mine, I'm gonna let it shine.
- This little light of mine, I'm gonna let it shine
- Let it shine, let it shine, let it shine.

I wasn't raised a Catholic. The school was close to our apartment and within easy walking distance for a 5-year-old. Later, I attended a Lutheran church and was confirmed Lutheran. As an adult, I worked my way through various denominations. Eventually, I became a believer in the manifestations of God's Spirit on this earth.

I've always felt a spiritual presence in my life, even in the early days of childhood. At age 32, I had an epiphany and suddenly knew God. I wrote about this story online[1].

I have witnessed firsthand instant healings, which cannot be explained from a physical perspective. They only make sense from a spiritual point of view.

Many things on this earth defy human understanding. One of them is the unique human body we walk around in and often take for granted. Even with the best of medical science, we are barely scratching the surface in understanding the workings of our brains.

When I encountered double vision from the high blood pressure, I was reintroduced to the design of our eyeballs. It is amazing how the brain pulls together both eyeball images and produces a single image. Now, my body is regenerating, and the two eyeball images are slowly getting back into sync.

All of this is to say that you cannot ignore spiritual realities in your quest for healing after receiving a doctor's death diagnosis. There is a spiritual aspect to our bodies that is not fully understood. It explains how placebos can work on 50% of people. It explains spontaneous healings that take place. It explains how people with severe addictions can simply stop in a moment in time, when God's Spirit touches their hearts.

Even without understanding God, it is okay to let healing music and scriptures feed your soul. So, engage your spiritual side to help heal your body.

My first big adventure into healing happened when I was only 5 years old. And even though I can't remember what took place, I am sure I had a heart-to-heart conversation with God on a sacred day in 1951. It is why I believe Scripture when it says in ancient texts.

"O Lord my God, I cried out to You,

And You Healed me." Psalms 30:2 NKJV

There are many comforting scriptures in the Bible. An excellent place to start reading and meditating is Psalms 34. It is a favorite of mine.

HOSPITALS

The only time I was ever in the hospital was when I was eight and found myself with appendix problems. It was removed in 1954. It was considered a disposable organ and not understood until recently. It is an overused surgery and is estimated to occur 36 more times[2] than actual appendicitis occurs. Like the gall bladder, it is another reservoir. This one helps our body's immune system by storing good bacteria used in our microbiome when the body needs it. Still, it is not fully understood by medical professionals.

Gall bladder surgery is another one of the most needless surgeries being done. Yes, you can live without a gall bladder. But you'll need to offset your fat intake with nutrients or drugs for life if you get it taken out. On the other hand, you can usually do a gall bladder cleanse to resolve gall stones. Search "gall bladder cleanse."

DENTISTS

The dentist's office is another story. Around the age of 12, my teeth were terrible. Contributing factors included too much sugar intake, and poor dental hygiene, like brushing after meals. When I was in the Navy, I had a lot of dental repairs done. I think that if it wasn't for Navy dentists, I might not have any teeth. They didn't like to take teeth out, so some teeth were rebuilt from the gums up. I'm not sure there isn't some genetic issue involved. My kids and grandkids have had some enamel issues. In any case, I've had a lot of work done on my teeth. I've had all the amalgam fillings removed. In their place are composite fillings. I believe removing the infected root canal tooth leaves me with no more root canal teeth. My dentist has confirmed that reality. I've had porcelain overlays on the top of my front teeth, and the new bridge I will get will have four new porcelain-crowned teeth. The front and rear teeth are anchored by existing teeth to the upper jaw.

Of course, I am diligent about taking care of my teeth now. I just can't remember how it all got started in my youth, albeit it's obvious I didn't take care of my teeth.

I've already mentioned the dangers of root canals and amalgam fillings. Take care of these issues, as they may negatively impact your health.

BODY'S ENERGETIC SYSTEM

Our bodies radiate energy outward, which can be observed with instruments. I'm about a year and a half into wearing a stem cell patch at the base of my neck. I'm wearing an X39 stem cell patch from a company called Lifewave[3]. It uses patented photo technology to reflect back into the body a frequency associated with increasing the body's copper peptides. It elevates the copper peptide levels, and this creates more new stem cells. The new stem cells can adapt to any body part or cell that needs help restoring or regenerating health.

I was in some accidents in my thirties. It left me with a loose spine. My lower back and neck would easily go out, and I would get terrible mid-back pain. The stem cell patch tightened up my spine and surrounding muscles. It eliminated my mid-back pain. For decades, I would twist my low back to adjust the spine, and I would adjust my neck by twisting it. Not any more. My spine is now like before the accidents, and I have no explanation for the physical improvement other than the X39 patch usage.

When I relocated my business office in 2003, I was left with both hands disabled. I could not open them for 2-3 weeks from being overused during the move. Once the hands were free to open, I was left with trigger fingers on the middle finger of each hand. My right hand resolved itself within a few weeks or months. My left hand never did. For 18 years, I could not close my left hand without the middle finger locking. It was painful to unlock the finger. After 6-9 months of being on the X39, my finger started to heal. I can now close and form a fist with my left hand.

Trigger fingers are relatively common. Surgeons can cut the tendon that snags and locks the finger. I don't believe in needless surgeries, and since it did not affect my typing, I didn't give it a second thought. The one person close to me that had the surgery wound up with a severe infection. He had to have his whole hand cut open to deal with it.

Regarding the mid-back pain, a stretch I started doing may have helped that issue. I'm just not sure. I'm also not sure what else the X39 is doing for me. However, I believe the low back, neck, and finger were healed because of this new stem cell photo-optical healing technology.

NUISANCE HEALTH ISSUES

We all live with specific disabilities, limitations, or health issues that might affect some activities. One of the issues for me has been a right wrist that gives out on me at times when pressure is applied. It can be pretty painful and first happened when I was in the Navy at age 21. Nothing could be found, and it has been a problem throughout my life. Well, guess what? No pushups, pull-ups, or other exercises or use of my right hand that requires a fully functioning wrist. One that has strength and won't just give away. Yes, it's painful when it acts up. But again, it doesn't affect my ability to type and write.

Other people have trick knees that give away at random times. I'm sure there are countless nuisance health issues we face during our lives. Yet no nuisance health issues will kill us. Just make sure whatever it is that you are living with is not changing or getting worse.

EARTHING

Another habit I recently adopted is earthing, aka grounding. I use two grounding pads. One at the computer in my office. A second at the chair I used to write at in the upper level of my home. All that is required is to be barefooted and place my feet on the pads. This allows a flow of electrons into my body to help repair electron-deficient cells. I do this almost daily for at least a couple of hours or more. There are a variety of grounding devices and even bed sheets that allow the benefit of grounding while you sleep. If you are seriously ill, this low-cost health strategy can help restore the health of body cells that need electrons.

MULTIVITAMINS

This may sound strange but I consider myself fortunate as a 24-year-old getting out of the Navy in 1970 to find no jobs in the Minneapolis electronics industry. I had worked on Naval weapons systems and had acquired an excellent technical background. At that time, there was 13% unemployment in the electronics industry. However, I found a group of unemployed engineers and technicians selling Nutralite household products door-to-door. I bought the sales kit and started knocking on doors. I had a wife, two kids, and a house mortgage. I needed an income to pay the bills.

A lot of the products were easy to sell. However, the kit contained two cases of Nutralite XXX Multivitamins. It was a two-month supply. The price was around $30/

month to consume these multivitamins. At the time, an excellent job paid $4/hour. I remember thinking, who pays $30 for multivitamins every month?

The short end of this story is that I never sold them and instead accepted a job with RCA to service TVs. I decided not to waste the multivitamins but to consume them. At 25, I thought I was in good health with plenty of energy. I had never taken a vitamin before this time. As I consumed this multivitamin, I was amazed at how much better I began to feel. I consumed the two-month supply I had. And, ever since then, I have taken nutraceuticals. Today, I wouldn't think twice about spending $40 a month on a good multivitamin.

That was how I started taking vitamins and other nutraceuticals. It was a blessing to me to be unemployed when I got out of the Navy. I may never of had the nutrient experience without it.

If you've never taken a good multivitamin, I recommend you try one. Vitacost.com has a good multivitamin for men and women at around $40 a month. I would suggest you try the Synergy brand without iron unless you need to take iron.

FISHBONE ANALYSIS

In quality engineering work, there is something called a fishbone diagram. It is used to find the cause of specific problems or to trace events. I had left the Navy, and I was unemployable in my electronics field. I found a group of unemployed engineers and technicians selling Nutralite products. I decided to join them. I sold Nutralite products.

I didn't sell their vitamins. I consumed the vitamins. I then felt better. I continued using vitamins throughout my life. If one event does not occur, the path that led me to where I am concerning my intake of nutraceuticals is broken, and a different history takes place. The fishbone diagram looks like the illustration below. This is a very simplified fishbone. It could be drawn in a more detailed way. You get the picture, right? There is a cause and effect. If any event is missed, the historical results are changed. You can use this technique to think about your death diagnosis. To analyze the path you've been on or the path you intend to go on.

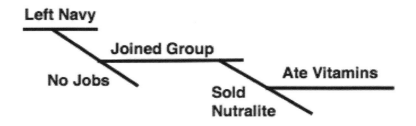

Fishbone Diagram

MAGNESIUM

After getting onto a good multivitamin, I think the next surprise for me was Doctor Whitaker's magnesium advice. This was my first experience with an alternative doctor's newsletter. He recommended 1,000 mg and six glasses of water daily for my low back pain. I've already discussed this earlier. Not only did it work immediately on me, but it has also worked on all my friends with whom I shared the advice.

The recommendation shocked me. I was already taking a good multivitamin. When I looked for the extent of magnesium, I found only 10 mg. I've been taking a magnesium supplement ever since. However, taking too much of this nutrient will result in loose stools.

CANCEROUS GROWTHS

One cancer cure I found during my first wife's death diagnosis was vitamin B17. Remember that G. Edward Griffin, in 1952, wrote: "A World Without Cancer[4] - The Story Of Vitamin B17" (deficiency).

Vitamin B17 is found in the seeds of all fruits. That includes apple seeds, cherry seeds, etc. However, the easiest way to consume B17 is by eating apricot seeds. You can buy them in one or two-pound bags. See informcentral.org for a place to buy them.

When Griffin came out with this cancer cure, an all-out assault took place on the consumption of B17 seeds. It is a fact that if you eat too many apricot seeds, they can make you sick. B17 releases cyanide into cancer cells to kill them. You can watch the "World Without Cancer" video to fully understand the mechanism of killing cancer cells. However, it appears safe to consume 1 apricot seed per 10 pounds of body weight. This is a safe protocol to use. With a person weighing 200 pounds, this means taking a maximum of only 20 seeds per day. A maximum hourly intake should only be 7 seeds.

Well, I got Jackie on the seeds. I held a weekly Bible study with three other people, and all four of us also started taking the apricot seeds using this protocol. I had a black crusty growth on my right leg. Two of my friends had similar growths. All three of us had these growths fall off and disappear. Jackie couldn't tolerate the seeds.

Eating the apricot seeds tasted like bitter cherry, and eating 7 seeds at a time could briefly numb the tongue. If you eat apples, you should also eat the apple seeds. Make sure you bite open the seeds, so the B17 is exposed. Otherwise, the apple seeds may just pass through your system.

I have had two more episodes over a decade later where this growth started again in the exact location. When the black growth fell off, I was left with what appeared as a birthmark on my right leg. When the area started to grow outward again, I scrapped it off using a pumice pad in the shower. It's gone, and I now regularly use aloe vera gel on the spot. It has returned to just looking like a birthmark.

When I first heard about this B17 cure, it was from a cancer patient that cured his cancer by eating apple seeds. He was so excited that he started promoting his cancer cure. The medical industry and government lawyers went right after him to shut him down. They did, and they also put him in jail on a technicality for not obeying the judge. You can still buy apricot seeds[5].

It is claimed that eating seven apricot seeds a day is an

excellent preventative tactic against getting cancer. It is also said that farm jams used to contain crunched-up fruit seeds and used to give us this B17 protection. In any case, I believe in Griffin's B17 approach to killing cancer.

MOVE IT OR LOSE IT

The old adage of "move it or lose it" is true from my experience. I've had substantial pain in four areas of my body. In every instance, the cause was the insufficient movement of some body muscle. The areas of pain were:

1) Left Arm/Forearm
2) Left Thigh/Hamstring
3) Left Knee/I.T. Band
4) Right Arm/Shoulder

Enter a young Chiropractor that specializes in sports medicine. This fellow was not good at therapy but had excellent diagnostic abilities. Having gone to chiropractic services, I was not interested in multiple treatments. So, I described my pain and asked what I needed to do. I told him he had only one time to help me on this issue.

Chiropractors can have you go for appointments every few days to get adjusted. This might make sense if you are too lazy to do your part of the healing and exercise. However, without physical activities, your body won't heal as fast. It's not the Chiropractor's duty to heal your body. They are there to assist in your healing.

#1. After my low back accident, I went to a Chiropractor 2-3 times a week for three years. During those three years, he adjusted my low back and neck. The pain relief was temporary and didn't last long. I eventually tried a home neck traction unit. After 20 minutes of using the neck traction, I had more relief than three years of neck adjustments by a Chiropractor.

So I stopped by this young Chiropractor and told him about the pain in my left arm. The pain radiated down my arm and was mainly a nuisance in my left forearm. Note: this was only arm pain, and no chest pain was present. Left arm pain is indeed associated with heart attacks. It was a different kind of pain. I asked what I needed to do to get rid of the pain.

After examining my arm and back, he diagnosed me with a tight horizontal muscle behind my left shoulder. He gave me a stretching exercise to do. The muscle involved was stretched and then became more flexible. Once that happened, the pain was totally gone.

#2. I have a regularly occurring pain under my left thigh. The problem is a tight hamstring muscle. To get relief is a simple matter of stretching my left hamstring muscle. Alternatively, you can place a tennis ball under the area where the pain is to stretch the muscle.

REFERRED PAIN

Often, the pain has nothing to do with where it is felt. In this case, it is called "referred pain." In all four examples I am illustrating, the pain was caused by another body part. Often, some distance away from where the pain was being felt.

———————

#3. I can get pain on the outside of my left knee. The pain has nothing to do with the knee. A long tendon called the I.T. band stretches from the buttocks area and attaches to the leg below the knee. When this long tendon gets tight, it rubs on the bone outside of the knee. A giveaway that this tendon is too tight is that, when you are walking, your feet will be pointed outward. When you walk, your feet should be pointed forward. You can find I.T. Band stretching exercises on YouTube. The stretch is similar to stretching the hamstring, and the pain disappears immediately.

#4. I could not raise my right arm over my head without incurring some serious shoulder pain. Note: If you get dizzy raising your right arm over your head, it can be a sign of heart problems. This was not the issue I was experiencing. Again, the solution was stretching my arm to loosen up a tight muscle/nerve issue behind my right shoulder area.

I've done much computer work over the last twenty years, which has limited my physical movements. The lesson is to keep moving your body unless you want more pain in your life.

BODY'S FASCIA LAYER

"Fascia[6] is a system of connective tissue that encases our body parts and binds them together. Fascia, made primarily of collagen, can be thought of as a sausage casing for your body's tissues. It surrounds muscles, nerves, tendons, and ligaments and gives them shape. Fascia also connects your skin to the tissue that is directly beneath it."

The fascia can be thought of as a lubricant for the movement of our muscles and limbs. You can find a YouTube video that explains this. In an hour-long documentary on the fascia, an experiment was done where an arm was not moved for 3-4 weeks. During that time, the fascia dried up and inhibited the arm's free movement. It took some effort to get the arm back in working condition.

There is a good reason why, when we don't exercise, our body stiffens up and results in pain. It's called the body's fascia layer. "Move it or lose it" was not just an old wive's tale. There is a physical reason for this advice. No one is going to exercise for you or keep your body moving. You'll just have to build some movement into your life to avoid a shoulder from locking up or other health issues caused by lack of use or movement.

STOMACH ISSUES
ACID REFLUX
BETAINE HCI

Stomach acid or "acid reflux" is an interesting health issue. If you listen to most doctors, they'll prescribe an acid reducer medication. However, alternative doctors will tell you that it isn't too much acid that is the real issue. It is a lack of sufficient acid in the stomach that is the cause of acid reflux. So is it really not enough stomach acid that is the cause of acid reflux?

How can that be? When stomach acid is low, the Lower Esophageal Sphincter valve[7] (LES) will relax allowing stomach acid to enter the esophagus. Then it is acid reflux time. This is another health irony that won't catch up to many doctors for another decade until 2032. This assumes that the LES valve muscle is healthy.

A natural product called Betaine, Betaine HCI, or Betaine HCI with Pepsin can be used to increase stomach acid. This product is created from sugar beets. I've now had over 12 years of experience using Betaine to increase the acid in my stomach.

About 12-14 years ago, I started having stomach and other health issues. The most significant problems were I started having brittle fingernails, an itchy rectum, and trouble when trying to swallow proteins. After some research, I discovered the cause was low stomach acid. I observed that I had some of the low acid symptoms[8] listed below.

Low Acid Symptoms

1) Bloating, belching, and flatulence.
2) Bad breath.
3) Diarrhea, or constipation.
4) Undigested food in the stool may occur.
5) Rectal itching.
6) Allergies to various foods.

7) Heartburn or GERD.

8) Dilated blood vessels in the nose.

9) Feeling hungry all the time.

My stomach issues continue today, and I consume 1-2 betaine capsules daily. I do not have enough stomach acid when I try to eat. Food seems to get stuck in the middle of my chest. When this happens, I take a betaine nutraceutical along with some water to increase the acid in my stomach.

After five minutes rest, I can continue eating without further difficulties. I sometimes have some allergic reactions, causing phlegm to come up from the stomach. I'm now thinking I should be taking two betaines instead of just one when I eat. Especially if I'm eating proteins.

In theory, Betaine can rebuild stomach acid. I have days that I don't use any Betaine. I'm not journaling this stomach and food issue. If I did, I might learn more about what is going on. I'm getting by on my current routine, but I admit I'm missing something.

I've found out that taking ginger reduces acid reflux by helping to heal the LES valve. I don't have a severe acid reflux issue but have had the issue pop up late at night. I also admit that it is difficult to discern when to add the acid, so this has been somewhat of a guessing game. Still,

I've learned something important about the low stomach acid being the cause.

Early on, when I got acid reflux late at night, I decided to take a betaine and add some acid. Suddenly, the symptoms worsened, and I panicked, thinking I had too much acid and now added more. I eventually learned to hang in there for 3-5 minutes and allow the LES to adjust. Then, all the symptoms of acid reflux just disappeared. In my case, I've absolutely confirmed that low stomach acid is the cause of acid reflux.

If this happens just before I go to bed, I might choose to kill off the acid with Mylanta. However, our bodies need stomach acid for proper digestion. I do get tired of fighting my body and, for that matter, having to think about what's happening.

The stomach is suppose to rebuild its cells every five weeks. So, I'm puzzled by why I've had to live with the issue for at least 12 years. There is probably a better betaine protocol out there I could follow. Your doctor can measure stomach acid. The lesson here is that acid-reducing drugs are not necessarily the fix for acid reflux.

MICROBIOME

When you take probiotics, you are adding good bacteria

to your intestines. When you eat prebiotics[9], like a green banana, or chicory root, you are feeding the good bacteria in your intestines. Collectively, everything living in your intestines is known as the microbiome.

This includes good bacteria, harmful bacteria, and many different viruses. It is estimated that we have 380 trillion microorganisms in our body, which has only 50-100 trillion cells[10]. Our bodies share life with other organisms, designed to help us. Our bodies also share a more significant microbiome from the earth.

Some alternative doctors believe that all disease starts in your gut's microbiome. For example, suppose your intestines get overwhelmed with harmful bacteria. In that case, it can result in C-diff[11], a deadly bad-bacterium disease. Your microbiome should be in good shape if you eat many vegetables and fruits. If you have any doubt, you should take probiotics to increase the good bacteria in your intestines. You can feed your microbiome by using prebiotics like green bananas and other foods that your good bacteria like to feed on. Search on prebiotics for a list of foods your good bacteria like to feed on.

For many years, I would get eye migraines. When I started using a probiotic formula, my eye migraines stopped in two weeks. The whole story of my eye migraines is discussed below.

* * *

BRAIN CELLS

It has recently been discovered that our brains also have a microbiome[12]. The microorganisms inside our gut's microbiome are the same as those inside our brains.

If that isn't strange enough, it has also been found that our hearts contain brain cells[13]. This gives new meaning to the phrase "Please take it to heart." It might be a good test of your doctor's knowledge to query them on these two recent medical discoveries. Does your doctor know about the brain's microbiome? What about the heart's brain?

CLARITY OF THOUGHT

Suppose you are a vegetarian or over age 50. In that case, you are most likely not getting the Vitamin B12 your body needs for clarity of thought. Vitamin B12 also affects the energy levels in your body. Low levels of this nutrient have also had seniors diagnosed with Alzheimer's.

If I need mental clarity, I take B12 and a Choline and Inositol nutrient mix. These two, along with essential fatty acids, keep me thinking clearly. The brain is 60%

fat[14] and needs to maintain that fat level for clear thinking.

MIBRAINES
EYE MIGRAINES

I experienced severe migraines when I was in my 30s, mainly on weekends. I was going too fast in life mentally during the week. When I got to the weekend and tried to slow my brain and body down, I wound up with terrible migraines centered in my forehead.

My favorite author is Norman Vincent Peale. In one of his books, he wrote about his experience with migraines. One day, he decided he shouldn't have to put up with them, so he told the migraines to leave him and stop. He claimed it worked, so I did the same thing, and my migraines also disappeared. I don't fully understand how this happens, although I realize there is a solid mind-body connection.

However, while I've never suffered from migraines after that time, I have experienced "eye migraines" on and off. I believe they started in my mid-50s while writing my first book.

Eye migraines usually begin as a tiny circle in the

middle of the left or right eye. As it progresses, the circle widens and eventually shifts to a letter "C" shape. Often, it's hard to figure out which eyeball is involved until it widens out. At that point, the "C" will move out towards the eye's outer edge. If it looks like "C," it is the left eye. If the "C" appears reversed, it is the right eye. As the circle or "C" expands, it blurs the image the eye sees. It can appear jagged or even have a color associated with them. For years, I thought that the vitreous humor of the eyeball had not separated from the retina. This can have a similar appearance. Note: This is normal as we age.

For years, I had taken all kinds of nutraceuticals, including the eye nutrients[15] from Dr. Whitaker that allowed me to stop using glasses for driving at age 60. However, I had not taken a probiotic product. When I started taking a good probiotic, my eye migraines stopped entirely in two weeks.

This isn't the end of this story, though. I had gotten lazy about taking other nutrients. Though I took the eye nutrients and probiotics, the eye migraines returned. It took me some time to figure this out, but it turns out that magnesium was the ingredient I also needed to stop the eye migraines. It was being taken when I first took the probiotics. The lesson I learned here is that sometimes there is synergy between nutrients that is not present when taken by themselves.

* * *

JOURNALING

I have kept a journal of eye migraines dating back at least ten years. I started the journal because I wanted to understand what was happening with my eyes. I have continued it throughout my double vision event. The bottom line is that it is difficult to understand what is going on with your health unless you are journaling about it. You need to record what is happening and not rely on your mind to recall events. The mind is not a good location to rely upon for remembering events. It also tends to recycle information around until you deal with it. In the process, it consumes more mental energy than is needed. It is best to do a brain dump of things you want to remember. You can place the information into a planner or other software device. You can also easily create notes on computers.

I use a Mac and have a planner called "Daylite[16]." I make all my brain dump notes on this software and do not rely on my brain to remember important data or events. I have a journal (a Daylite note) named "Eye Health-Ed's." Recent journal entries, during my double vision, look like this.

* * *

Eye Journal Sample Entries

7/1 - I have experienced some left eyeball pain on and off. Nothing consistently. Some tightness at the very top and rear of my skull on occasion. Again, nothing consistent. Seems like eye migraines have increased after probiotics absence.

7/1 - Blood pressure has dropped back to the 133/76 range after using olive leaf extract and celery seed extract.

- 7/4 - Right eye - 12:46 am
- 7/6 - Left eye - 8:15 pm

BLOOD PRESSURE NORMALIZED

7/11 - Blood Pressure at rest 116/70 - 70 bpm

After three weeks on Olive Leaf Extract and Celery Seed Extract. This is the lowest blood pressure I can recall.

End Of Journal Sample Entries

* * *

If you want to understand what is happening with your health or how a death diagnosis affects your body, start journaling. Get a small empty journal and start writing, or use a convenient software program. The entry on 7/4 records a right eye migraine; on 7/6, a left eye migraine is recorded. Anything that affects my eyes is documented in this journal. Recording these events as they occur is the best practice to document a health issue. However, from a practical standpoint, I often write the event on a piece of paper and then add it to my journal as soon as possible. Smartphones can also offer a quick event capture method. On my iPhone, I simply say: "Hey Siri, create a new note."

AMINO ACIDS

There are 20 amino acids[17] that our bodies use, which are the building blocks of proteins. 9 of these are essential to the body's health, and 11 are non-essential. You cannot expect health without making sure you are getting the essential amino acids that your body needs. If unsure of your intake, you can supplement with a product like Sun Chlorella[18], which has a good amino acid content.

* * *

ENZYMES

Unless you eat a lot of fresh vegetables and fruits, your body may not get the enzymes your body needs. Our bodies will manufacture enzymes, but it is estimated that 50% of what our bodies needs comes from the foods we eat. Modern farming and food processing methods are killing off the enzymes in the foods we eat. Unless we buy directly from a farm we trust, we are no longer getting nutrient-dense foods. Several nutraceutical products are filling the gap on amino acids and enzymes. I choose to supplement with an enzyme product.

If you suffer from digestive problems, a supplemental enzyme product[19] may be the answer you are looking for.

SLEEP ISSUES

My first significant lesson on sleep was learning to use a pillow between my knees. I had my low back go out from accidents. When I slept, one knee would overlap the other, and my low back would go out again.

Sleeping can be hazardous. I've lost track of issues I woke up with that did not exist when I went to bed. I tend to sleep on my left side. It requires that I do some offsetting exercise. I use some foam at the bottom of the bed. This keeps the weight of the blankets off my feet.

Getting in a good walk during the day always helps me sleep. Taking magnesium and other minerals before going to bed also helps me sleep. There is a massive amount of advice about sleeping online.

SENSITIVE SKIN
BACK ARM SKIN RASH
BABYFACE

I have had several people ask me what I use on my face. I don't look 76. I look more like a 55-65-year-old. I've even had a friend tell me that I have a baby face regarding my skin. Other than nutrients, I've done two specific things.

As a young man of about 30, I stopped using alcohol-based after-shave lotions. Instead, I use aloe vera gel for my face and hair. After that is dry, I use a moisturizer cream on my face and neck. I've just started taking a collagen nutrient, which might help soon.

My skin used to be extremely sensitive to touch, and sometimes I experienced pain when touched. This skin sensitivity disappeared after I added alpha lipoic acid to my nutrient regimen. I also used to get a rash or bumps behind my arm. These went away when I added essential fatty acids to my nutrients.

ELECTROMAGNETIC POLLUTION
DANGERS OF 5G

There is little question in my mind that 5G towers are dangerous. I used to work on radars in the Navy, and the frequencies being used by 5G are also used in military crowd control machines. These frequencies can penetrate the skin and alter the body's health. If I lived near a 5G tower, I would be concerned.

Frequencies by themselves might be inconsequential. A power factor (watts) affects how dangerous EMFs are. Having said that, some people now have many health issues around the massive EMFs present. It will only increase as 5G continues to roll out. If you have unexplained sickness, you should check whether your health is influenced by 4G or 5G radiation.

Now, devices can neutralize the EMF radiation found in your home or office environment. Search the internet using the phrase "EMF neutralizer."

The electrical wires in our homes pick up EMF radiation. The electrical wiring will then function like a transmitter and radiate EMF energy into the rooms of our home. If your bed is next to electrical outlets, this radiated energy, aka "dirty electricity," can affect your sleep and health. Stetzer Electric, Inc. has developed an outlet filter called a STETZERIZER. It is a modular device that plugs into electric outlets. By deploying these filters throughout your home, you can eliminate or reduce the effects of the dirty electricity in your environment. An outlet meter is available to verify the efficacy of the filters.

BODY ENERGY

The best nutrient I discovered for our body's energy is "Guarana" in 1200 mg doses. Guarana is an ancient herb used for centuries. It is similar to caffeine but natural to the body. There are other nutrients that your body needs for your energy levels[20]. I have used guarana for five decades.

ANXIETY

The best nutrient I discovered for anxiety is the herb, Kava Kava. This herb may cause adverse health issues if used with alcohol. It shouldn't be taken if you are drinking alcohol. I take 2-4 Kava pills at 500 mg/each. As I discussed earlier, I don't have much anxiety, but it has happened. Kava is also said to be a muscle relaxer.

STOP THINKING AT NIGHT

GABA[21], an amino acid, is the best nutrient to relax my brain from thinking when I want to sleep. It is a neurotransmitter known as gamma-aminobutyric acid. I take GABA in 500 mg doses. It always helps to slow my brain down. It can also relieve dry coughs.

The second nutrient to have on hand is L-Theanine[22]. It works like GABA and helps quiet the mind.

SMARTPHONE
HABIT TRACKERS

This strategy returns to the prior discussion of "Don't Expect What You Don't Inspect." There are now a variety of apps for smartphones that will allow you to track your daily habits and routines. I found several for the iPhone. Some habit trackers want an annual or monthly fee. Depending on features, some have an initial cost of $5 to $50. However, I found a free app called "Habbity" for the iPhone. I'm not sure how long it will stay that way. It seems to have all the functionality I want in a habit tracker.

When you enter something to track, the input screen looks like the first screen image. This app screen allows you to input items. It even graphs your progress for you.

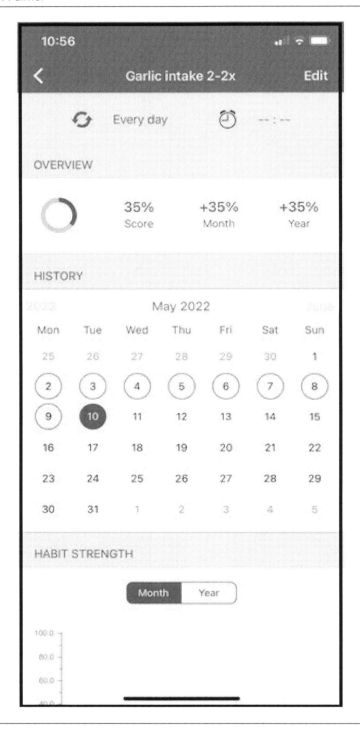

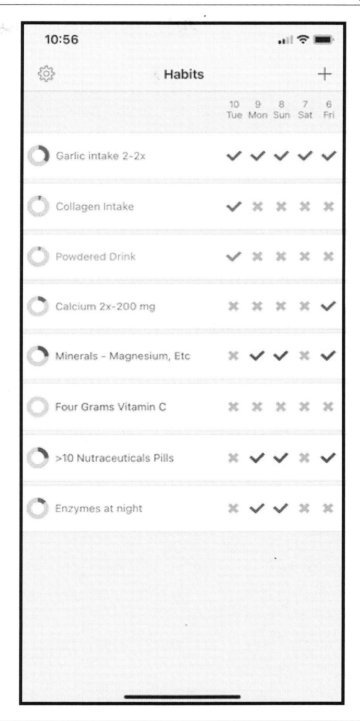

The second screen-shot is what shows up when the app is launched. I've added eight items to track. The screen presents the dates of the current week. If you've done the event or habit, you simply touch the day, and it places a check mark showing completion. The top item, garlic intake, shows I completed this habit all seven days this week. The circles on the left show your week's progress. If you open the detailed panel, circles show the completions.

Maybe you are too sick to track your intake of nutrients and have a family member helping you. They can keep track of details for you, including journaling what is happening to you. Be sure you have an honest conversation about what you are experiencing.

BIG PHARMA DRUGS / MEDS

I believe there are natural solutions for every single pharmaceutical drug offered by allopathic medical doctors. Drugs are what traditional doctors are trained to dispense. Drugs are designed to mask symptoms and are not meant to resolve underlying health conditions. There is a profit motive to keep you on drugs. You'll need to think outside the box to find other non-drug solutions to health problems.

Search the internet using the phrase, "alternative to _____ (name of your drug)." You might be surprised. You can also search the internet using the phrase, "alternative cures for _____ (name of your disease, illness, or health issue)."

———————

CHAPTER ELEVEN
Death Vs. Healing

"I call heaven and earth as witnesses today

against you, *that* I have set before you

life and death, blessing and cursing;

therefore choose life, that both you and

your descendants may live;" Deut. 30:19

When it comes to a doctor's death diagnosis, there are two profound beliefs you must possess inside your mind. **First**, you must honestly have something to live for and to look forward to. Maybe it is living long enough to see a grandchild get married. Perhaps it is to live long enough to see a great-grandchild be born. Maybe it is to reach some goal you've been working on for years.

Second, and it might be even more critical, you must believe your body can heal.

I was inspired to write this book when a friend of mine announced she was diagnosed with ALS. This meant she might have only 2-5 years to live and could die an excruciating death.

What inspired me to write was not the death diagnosis but that she would follow the doctor's advice to her death. Allopathic doctors don't believe there is a cure for ALS and many other diseases. Of course, this is what they impart to their patients. "Well ... it's your DNA, and in your genes. Sorry!" I can just imagine the dialogue. The first decision that must be made is that the doctor's opinion doesn't have to be your reality.

The second decision is your DNA is not in control of your destiny for the reasons I've already mentioned in this book. So here are four things to remember.

1. Have something to live for.
2. Realize your body can heal.
3. The doctor is entitled to his opinion.
4. The doctor's opinion doesn't have to become your reality.

I was reminded again today of all the spontaneous healings that occur. You could spend a lifetime researching this information. I have witnessed miraculous healings. Still, it starts with having something to live for and then believing in the possibility your body can be healed.

After Jackie died of pancreatic cancer, I contacted an acquaintance of mine named Caroline. She had cancer, and I was excited to share some of the cancer cure information I had found. Caroline wasn't the slightest bit interested in any healing. She said: "Oh, Ed, I'm not interested in getting cured. Quite frankly, the pull from the other side is stronger than the pull from this side. I'm just trying to prepare my kids for my exit."

Sometimes it is not about wanting to be healed. Maybe, it's because death is accepted, and now you don't want to disappoint anyone by trying to live instead? That sounds strange, doesn't it?

Vern, another friend, simply checked out (died) three days after discovering a tumor on his lower back meant he would not walk again. He had a tough life and was spiritually ready, just like Caroline said she was.

I saw my friend with ALS yesterday. It is now three years after the ALS diagnosis, and I thought she looked better than last year. I talked to her again about the healingals.org site I found. Her response was, "you can't heal ALS!" I don't believe that stuff on the internet. I said, "you don't have to believe it." Still, it won't hurt to check it out.

If you want to leave the planet, just stop eating and drinking. After a week, your body will start to shut down. After another week, you might experience your desire to exit the planet. You can live a long time without food, but a clock is running out of time if you stop drinking water or other liquids. Your body is estimated to be 60% water.

Shouldn't I believe My doctor?

My short answer is only a "Maybe." We have all been programmed from birth to believe the doctor. However, from my perspective, the answer would be, "Why should I believe the doctor, given historical medical facts?"

- Hospitals and doctors are dangerous to your health. The last place you should run to is where people are gathered together sick.

- Hospitals and doctors[1] are now the 3rd leading[2] cause of death in the USA. Estimated at 250,000 to 300,000 deaths per year by a John Hopkins study.

- Doctors did not take the time to understand the lungs of covid-19 patients leading to many deaths.

- It took over 100 years for most doctors to acknowledge that Vitamin C cured scurvy[3].

- Doctors were still performing lobotomies[4] three decades after it was known to damage the brain.

- 90% of all doctors work in corporations, and they

are tightly controlled by standardized medical procedures. If they stray from these procedures, they can lose their medical licenses.

◆ Doctors who speak out against a standard treatment protocol can lose their medical licenses.

◆ Allopathic medicine is controlled by Big Pharma and is designed primarily to dispense drugs.

◆ Doctor-prescribed drugs only mask symptoms. They do not fix the underlying health conditions.

◆ Doctors are not trained in nutraceutical healing unless they've left conventional medicine.

◆ It takes 17 years for information to get to doctors who are too busy treating people to read studies.

◆ It is likely that your physician has not told you the truth about covid vaccines.

◆ It is likely that if you received the covid vaccine, you were not informed about the possibility of serious adverse events. See full article[5] here.

◆ Doctors play whack a mole with symptoms. You can do your own guessing with a little effort.

I could write a book on the bad historical practices of the medical industry and its doctors. I don't want to write a screed, but you get the point, right? Why should you put your faith 100% in what really amounts to just a doctor's opinion? Why shouldn't you believe your body can be healed?

———

Jesus said: "If you can believe, all things are possible to him [or her] who believes." Mark 9:23

CHAPTER TWELVE
Healing Secrets & Tips

100 Healing Secrets Learned
From 50-Years Of Life Experiences

Here are 100 healing secrets learned from 50 years of experimenting with self-care for myself.

1. A doctor's death diagnosis is only an opinion.

2. A doctor's opinion doesn't have to become a reality.

3. Allopathic doctors operate under standard medical practices and can lose their medical licenses if they deviate from the procedures of their industry.

4. Allopathic doctors are not educated on alternative healing with nutrients. Their education is dictated by Big Pharma and is focused on dispensing drugs.

5. Every citizen should be able to trust the CDC, FDA, WHO, NIH, and every other three-letter government agency associated with our health and food safety. However, alternative health cures and nutraceutical treatments are now (2022) highly

censored and hidden from the general public.

6. Google and other major tech giants censor all medical information that does not comply with standardized medical treatment protocols.

7. Google and other major tech giants censor all medical narratives that challenge the government narratives presented by the CDC and FDA.

8. Everyone should take personal responsibility for their own health. Your health and healing are not the doctor's responsibility, regardless of your family's beliefs. Your choices about living or dying are yours alone!

9. Vaccines can have dangerous side effects, which should be adequately disclosed, so every patient can give their "informed consent."

10. Doctors and hospitals can be dangerous to your health and "medical errors" are now the third leading cause of death in the United States.

11. For every drug prescribed, there exists a health approach using nutrients and other alternative techniques for dealing with sickness and disease.

12. Allopathic medical doctors are trained to treat symptoms, not the underlying health cause.

13. Functional medical doctors seek to get to the bottom of health issues.

14. Integrative medical doctors use alternative health modalities like chiropractic services, massage therapies, nutrition, exercise, etc.

15. Naturopathic medical doctors recognize that health issues may result from mental health issues or other things like environmental influences.

16. Electroceutical medicine uses energy technology devices and frequencies to diagnose and treat diseases.

17. Orthomolecular medicine uses mega doses of nutrition and vitamins to effect healing in the body. Vitamin C, as an example, in large amounts can affect cures in cancer patients. Treatment protocols exist, including a sepsis[1] protocol using Vitamin C.

18. Many patients move from one doctor to another until they find one that can help. Why? It gets back to the medical education of the doctor. If you have a death diagnosis, you can choose to step out of standard medical practices and seek the help of an alternative medical doctor. Think outside the box!

19. Bad health habits are easy to get into, hard to get out of, and can lead to an early death.

20. Think habits, change habits!

21. Everyone lives with some type of health problem.

22. There is no proof that annual flu shots work.

23. Root canal teeth are dangerous to your health.

24. Amalgam dental fillings are dangerous to your health.

25. If you have an unexplainable disease, it may be related to your teeth or the environment you are living in.

26. Germ theory states that microbes are the cause of disease.

27. Terrain theory states that it is a weak immune system that causes disease.

28. Traditional medical insurance does not pay for your health needs. It pays for sickness treatment.

29. An alternative strategy is to invest in health needs like vitamins, minerals, and other nutraceuticals. In other words, spend your money on your body's terrain and not just on medical insurance in case you get sick. Actively plan to stay healthy.

30. When you invest in your health needs, you are investing in your body's terrain, and by doing so, you are increasing your immune system's disease resistance.

31. Suppose you just buy medical insurance and don't even take a multivitamin. In that case, you have to believe your body will get everything it needs from the food you eat. This is what is believed and

promoted by most allopathic doctors.

32. Given modern food processing, most foods are no longer nutrient dense. If you don't supplement with nutraceuticals, it is a good bet your body is deficient in essential nutrients like magnesium, vitamin C, vitamin D, etc.

33. It takes time for nutrients to build up in the body, and everyone's body has its own needs.

34. Bodies differ in nutrient needs because everyone has a different terrain or environment. One person might consume many vegetables and fruits, and another might consume hardly any.

35. There may be no need to take blood pressure lowering medications when olive leaf extract, celery seed extract, and bromelain can lower your blood pressure without medications' side effects.

36. There may be no need to take drugs to help with bowel movements. Increasing vitamin C or magnesium levels will reach a state of loose bowels and do the needed job.

37. Our bodies are energetic and can be diagnosed and treated with frequency devices. Every organ in our body has its own distinct frequency of vibration.

38. Our bodies need to be hydrated and have a fascia organ or system that uses water to lubricate our

muscles, etc. "Move It or Lose It" has a scientific basis. It's not just an old wive's tale.

39. You will have trouble moving joints if your body is not adequately hydrated. The old adage "move it or lose it" is a reality of a dried-up fascia system.

40. If you have pain, it may not be where it is felt. It might be referred pain caused by a problem far from where the pain is felt.

41. If you take responsibility for your own healing, it may be met with family resistance.

42. We've all been programmed to trust the doctors. Family members will pressure you to do what the doctor wants you to do.

43. If you spend two days researching your death diagnosis, you may know more about the subject than your doctor. Doctors do not have time to read studies because they are busy with appointments. Doctors don't spend time reviewing alternative healing tactics and methods. They could also get in trouble recommending alternative, nutrient, or nutraceutical treatments.

44. It took a long time to get a death diagnosis, and it will take some time to get out of it.

45. Your body wants to heal itself.

46. Genes do not determine your health. This is old

thinking. In the New Biology field, epigenetics has shown that the environment of your body and its nutrient intake can turn genes on and off as needed.

47. Your health is not trapped by your genetic code.

48. Your health is not trapped by damaged DNA, as it can repair itself.

49. Many needless surgeries are being done in the United States.

50. Before you get a gall bladder removed, try a gall bladder cleanse.

51. Your body rebuilds 95% of its cells within a year.

52. Before getting a joint replacement surgery, try feeding your joint the nutrients it needs to heal.

53. There are natural antibiotics the body can use without the side effects of drugs.

54. Your body has a microbiome that is responsible in large part for your state of health.

55. An estimated 380 trillion bacteria and viruses live in our body, which only has an estimated 50-100 trillion cells.

56. Viruses are often information cells that the body uses to update its defenses.

57. Diseases are hard to get into a body with a robust immune system.

58. Natural pain relief nutrients do not have the side effects of Big Pharma drugs or OTC products.

59. Human bodies do not make their own Vitamin C.

60. Covid health protocols require nutrient intake to strengthen the immune system and the body's terrain.

61. According to author Neville Goddard, emotional disturbances cause all diseases.

62. There are cancer cures over 70 years old that are ignored by allopathic medicine.

63. Dr. Edward Griffin gave us a cancer cure in the 50s using fruit seeds containing vitamin B17.

64. Dr. Johanna Budwig gave a cancer cure in the 50s using flaxseed oil mixed with organic 1% cottage cheese. The cottage cheese makes the flaxseed oil water soluble for easier absorption by the body.

65. There are an estimated 400+ alternative approaches to curing cancer. A lot of these are now documented in many books.

66. Cancer treatment is a multi-billion dollar business in allopathic medicine. Simple cures are not wanted or sought out by pharmaceutical firms.

67. Alternative cancer cures are being censored and hidden from public view by big tech. Big Pharma also floods the internet with negative gaslighting

on any alternative approach or treatment.

68. Blood pressure and cancers are silent killers.

69. Your body needs to live in the parasympathetic nervous system for healing in your body.

70. Buried trauma from our childhood can be the cause of various diseases. Buried traumas must be confronted and dealt with for healing to take place.

71. Buried trauma can have our bodies living in the sympathetic nervous system or in "fight or flight" mode. This can prevent our bodies from healing.

72. Our bodies have a spiritual component to healing, which shouldn't be ignored.

73. Forgiving others and yourself is a necessity if you want to achieve healing. This is part spiritual and part parasympathetic nervous system needs.

74. Without realizing it, given our actions and thoughts, we are where we are in life. Whatever is going on inside of our body is reflected outward.

75. People can get a "white coat syndrome" when going to a doctor or dentist, which can substantially raise their blood pressure.

76. Coffee can not only raise your blood pressure, but it can also deplete calcium from your body.

77. In the Bible, 70 years of age[2] is considered a good life.

78. 80 years of age is considered a strong life.

79. Genesis 6:3 suggests we can live to 120 years of life assuming we care for ourselves.

80. Lifewave (.com) manufactures a stem cell patch that can cause the body to create new stem cells. They also manufacture other phototherapy patches to help with other health conditions.

81. Other stem cell nutraceuticals like "Active Stem" are available.

82. Products are available to lengthen "Telomeres" in the body, extending cell life.

83. Prism glasses can offset eyeball tracking issues.

84. We must believe our bodies can heal if we have a death diagnosis.

85. We must have a reason to continue living.

86. Hospice care will help you stay as comfortable as possible on your way toward death. That is, they will help you die.

87. You may need someone to help you figure out how to stay alive if you are in hospice.

88. The brain has an organ that can keep us from learning the truth. See the reticular activating system discussion.

89. There is a mind-body connection that cannot be ignored regarding healing.

90. A mercury product, thimerosal, is used in many vaccine products. Aluminum is an adjuvant to activate vaccines. Both of these are neurotoxins.

91. Prostate PSA tests[3] are not reliable by themselves to cut out your prostate gland.

92. Medical lab results are notoriously off by 50%. If you have a negative lab report, you owe it to yourself to get another test from a different lab.

93. Covid PCR tests are inherently inaccurate and depend upon processing cycles. I would not personally use them, as the inventor claims they shouldn't be used for coronaviruses.

94. Colonoscopies are dangerous to your health when using a mechanical scope up the rectum. There are sanitation issues and known tears taking place. Instead, there is a non-invasive method that can be used. Listen to your body and observe your bowel movements for difficulty and blood.

95. Annual health and dental checks promote fear and the idea you can't take care of yourself without the doctor and dentist's yearly input. This belies the fact that for millennials, there were no such checks.

96. Hypnosis absolutely works. I have experienced it myself. It takes concentration to be hypnotized.

97. Self-hypnosis is an excellent way to influence the

subconscious mind to change habits.

98. Living in the present moment and mindfulness are valuable strategies to reduce stress in your life.

99. Meditation helps reduce stress in your life.

100. Prayer is similar to meditation and can improve your health in ways even the medical industry cannot understand. It's a spiritual mystery!

"I will meditate on Your precepts, and contemplate Your ways [God]." Psalms 119:15

———

62 Nutraceutical Secrets

1. Vitamin B5 can relieve allergies and sinus miseries.

2. Vitamin C can relieve allergies and sinus miseries. I currently take 5 grams daily. I have taken up to 23 grams in a single day. My body felt better at 12 grams. The exciting aspect of Vitamin C is that your body will tolerate it a lot more when you are sick. See prior Vitamin C discussions in this book.

3. Essential Fatty Acids (EFA) are anti-inflammatory.

4. Turmeric (Curcumin) is anti-inflammatory and is a known pain relief ingredient.

5. Borage Oil (GLA) is anti-inflammatory and is claimed to reduce the impact of arthritis. The GLA ingredient is also found in evening primrose oil.

6. Choline and Inositol can help your brain's clarity.

7. Coconut oil and other medium chain triglycerides have been shown to help the brain and even positively impact Alzheimer's patients. A patent exists from a doctor who healed her husband of this dreaded memory disease.

8. Betaine HCI can relieve acid reflux by adding acid.

9.   White Willow Bark Extract is a pain relief nutrient.

10. White Willow Bark is the basis of aspirin meds.

11. Boswellia (Indian Frankincense) is a pain nutrient.

12. Frankincense was one of the three gifts to Jesus.

13. Vitamin B6 is used in pain relief. If you take too much B6, you may experience tingling in your feet or hands. If so, you need to lower the intake level.

14. B6 can function as a natural diuretic to eliminate body fluids. I witnessed a woman get rid of her knee and ankle swelling within a few weeks. The doctor told her she had had rheumatoid arthritis for over four decades. B6 and stopping beer intake resolved her swelling issues.

15. GABA helps quiet the mind at night. I use a dosage of 500-1,000 mg.

16. GABA can also stop a dry cough. I use 500 mg.

17. L-Theanine is also helpful in quieting the mind at night. I use a dosage of 100 mg.

18. L-Tryptophan can help you get to sleep at night.

19. Valerian can help you stay asleep at night.

20. Melatonin can help you sleep at night. You can now find melatonin in 12-milligram pills. This is way too much to aid your sleep. If sleeping is your aim, try using a 1-milligram dose. A cancer protocol uses a 6-12 milligram dose, but this is not

recommended for sleeping difficulties. In fact, large amounts may work the opposite for sleeping.

21. St. John's Wort is used in pain relief and for nerves.

22. Alpha Lipoic Acid is the best nutrient for nerve issues (pain relief).

23. Serrapeptase is used for pain relief, especially for fibrinolytic proteins causing pain. It can also help dissolve or prevent blood clots.

24. There are 12 bone support nutrients discussed in this book.

25. Kava Kava is what I use for anxiety when it strikes. I use a dosage of 500 to 1,000 mg.

26. Suppose you don't know what nutrients you need for a health condition. In that case, an excellent place to start is with a pre-formulated nutraceutical.

27. If you dare to look outside of allopathic medicine for healing, look at alternative health doctors and alternative healing strategies for your disease.

28. It is estimated that 70% of adults are deficient in magnesium, which is used throughout the body.

29. If you have low back pain, you are most likely deficient in magnesium and may be dehydrated.

30. I take 200-400 mg of magnesium glycinate daily.

31. 90% of our day's activities are an automatic

response from the habits and routines located in our subconscious minds.

32. 10% of our day's activities are consciously decided.

33. Vitamin C can be taken in large quantities. See the Vitamin C protocol[1] on orthomolecular.org.

34. You will also find Vitamin C information[2] on the Orthomolecular.com website.

35. Vitamins come in various forms. Some are easier to consume or swallow than other forms.

- Tablets
- Caplets
- Capsules
- Powder
- Liquid
- Chewable's

36. I try to avoid tablets whenever possible. They are the hardest for me to swallow if they are larger than 1/4 inch in diameter. Capsules are easy, but if you are consuming a lot of them, you may want to change some of them to a powder or liquid form.

37. Vitamins are made of various ingredients, albeit most vitamins are synthetic.

- Synthetic
- Whole Food

- Fermented Whole Food

38. Fermented whole food vitamins are the most expensive and natural for the body.

39. Supplement needs for optimum health[3] are identified at the orthomolecular.com site.

40. Ph strips can measure the body's pH levels. A highly acidic body is open to disease. An alkaline body is resistant to disease.

41. Your belief can affect your healing. That is why 50% of people respond well to a sugar pill in drug efficacy tests.

42. A negative belief can accelerate your death. That is if you believe you will die, you will.

43. There are covid-19 healing protocols available.

44. When the government tested the efficacy of the military's drug stock after 30 years, they found that the drugs were still 90% or more effective. This means you should take expiration dates with a grain of salt. Your medicines and nutrients will probably last at least ten years. Don't be so quick to throw the nutrients or drugs away.

45. If you engage in self-care, you must pay attention to your body and what is happening.

46. Visually observing the color of your skin, eyes, fingernails, etc., can tell you a lot about the health

of your body.

47. YouTube has a lot of video tips on dealing with health issues.

48. Pinterest has a lot of image tips on dealing with health issues.

49. Don't search using Google for alternative health information. They have censored alternative health sites like greenmedinfo.com, a valuable alternative health information repository.

50. If your health battle winds up being a battle of willpower against your imagination, guess who wins? Yep, your imagination!

51. Just because professionals like nurses and doctors know what is healthy to do, it doesn't mean they'll do it. That is why many of them still smoke cigarettes.

52. Keep nutrients in front of your face; if you want to, make sure you take them daily.

53. Focus on what you can control when it comes to your health. Do what is in your power to do.

54. Create a simple chart to help track your performance while building a new habit.

55. Simple hydration tests such as pinching the skin on your hand and observing the color of your urine are helpful. Weight scales can also put a

microcurrent through your body while standing on a scale to give you a reading of body hydration.

56. Stay away from seed oils. They contain Omega 6 linoleic acid (LA) that cause inflammation in the body. The problem with Omega 6 fatty acids is that we are exposed to too many of them in modern foods. This distorts the ratio of Omega 3 to Omega 6 acids.

57. Gamma Linoleic acid (GLA) is also an Omega 6 essential fatty acid (EFA) but has been identified as very helpful to those suffering from arthritis.

58. Bromelain, which is a pineapple enzyme, is also reported to help people with arthritis. It is a known pain killer and has personally helped me.

59. Taking Bromelain with food aids in digesting the food. Taking Bromelain on an empty stomach can function as a pain killer for the body.

60. You have a health sandbox to play in when it comes to healing your body. Everything outside of allopathic medicine is in this sandbox. Let your imagination run wild, researching cures and thinking about how to heal your body. Add into your health sandbox anyone who can assist you in restoring your health.

61. If you are practicing a habit associated with your

doctor's death diagnosis, you must stop.

62. Your body wants to heal. All you have to do is feed it what it needs and stop doing anything destructive that harms your health.

———

The next list represents 17 warning signs to pay attention to, as they might be serious health issues. These body signs may require your immediate attention.

17 Health Concern Signs

1. Cracked, calloused skin
2. Black irregular skin growths
3. Yellowing skin
4. Edema or Swelling
5. Weak brittle finger nails
6. White spots on finger nails
7. Deformed finger nails
8. White finger nails
9. Itching anus
10. Bloody urine
11. Bloody stools
12. Bloody noses
13. Migraines
14. Weak erections
15. Yellowing eyes
16. Pain
17. Weakness in body

12 Alternative Doctors

1. Dr. Julian Whitaker

2. Dr. David Williams

3. Dr. Frank Schallenberger

4. Dr. Joseph Mercola

5. Dr. Al Sears

6. Dr. Steven Gundry

7. Dr. Bryan Ardis

8. Dr. Keith-Scott Mumby

9. Dr. Rand McClain

10. Dr. Mark Stengler

11. Dr. Rothfeld

12. Dr. Gerhauser

The above list represents alternative doctors that have provided health care inputs to me via emails, printed newsletters, alternative health eBooks, and print books. If you search their names, you'll find their websites and free newsletters you can subscribe to.

40 Alternative Websites

1) thedoctorsdeathdiagnosis.com

2) godshealingandcancer.com

3) godandhealing.org

4) informcentral.org

5) healthmeans.com

6) doctoryourself.com

7) drtenpenny.com

8) drnorthrup.com

9) drleemerritt.com

10) carriemadej.com

11) mercola.com

12) gundrymd.com

13) dailyhealthpost.com

14) healthrevelations.com

15) cancerdefeated.com

16) suzycohen.com

17) nutritionandhealing.com

18) frankshallenberger.com

19) allianceforadvancedhealth.com

20) naturalhealthresponse.com

21) newmarkethealth.com

22) greenmedinfo.com

23) thetruthaboutcancer.com

24) orthomolecular.org

25) theheartysoul.com

26) alternative-doctor.com

27) holisticbodyhealth.com

28) theartofantiaging.com

29) naturalhealth365.com

30) healthsecret.com

31) conqueringcancer.info

32) cancertruth.net

33) covid19criticalcare.com

34) americasfrontlinedoctors.org

35) dr-eva.com

36) foodrevolution.org

37) worldcouncilforhealth.org

38) childrenshealthdefense.org

39) nathancrane.com

40) www.vaccines.news

Notes

Introduction

1. Allopathic refers to traditional medical practices involved with the dispensing of drugs, surgery and radiation strategies for the treatment of the symptoms of illness. This is the traditional medical system, which is designed to focus treatment on symptoms instead of the underlying disease or health of the body.

2. To learn more about Orthomolecular Medicine and the use of vitamins and nutrition in the treatment of disease, go to www.orthomolecular.org. Additional information can be found at www.doctoryourself.com.

3. Naturopathy is the treatment of disease that seeks to avoid drugs and surgery in favor of emphasizing the use of natural agents like air, water, and herbs. Naturopathic doctors also use tissue manipulation and electrotherapy,

4. I.E. - America's #1 Guide To Natural Health reference book titled: "Prescription For Nutritional Healing" Fifth Edition or later by Author Phyllis A. Balch, CNC

5. Aspirin is a chemical drug manufactured and based on the natural pain killing effects of chemicals found in nature like those of Willow Bark Extract. Other natural pain killing nutrients like Boswellia or Frankicense also exist.

6. If you want to study the use of Vitamin C as a healing nutrient, you will find full details along with a suggested protocol for using Vitamin C at www.doctoryourself.com.

7. If you want to study the use of Vitamin C for healing cancer, you will find full details along with a suggested protocol for using Vitamin C at www.doctoryourself.com.

8. Details on the efficacy of Vitamin C used in China and other locations

can be found in the press releases of Orthomolecular Medicine. The press releases are located online at www.orthomolecular.org/resources/omns/. You can study Vitamin C for healing at this site and also at www.doctoryourself.com.

Anatomy Of A Health Crisis

1. https://www.frankshallenberger.com

The Health Crisis 2

1. www.alternative-doctor.com The comments here are from his March 1, 2022 health newsletter.

2. Found on page 6 of the 1944 book titled: "Feelings Are The Secret" by author Neville Goddard. This book is in the public domain and is widely available in print and eBook versions.

3. https://www.youtube.com/watch?v=QeYMduufa-E. You can also search on G. Edward Griffin or his book *The World Without Cancer*.

The Health Crisis 3

1. https://sciencebasedmedicine.org/are-medical-errors-really-the-third-most-common-cause-of-death-in-the-u-s-2019-edition/

2. https://www.hopkinsmedicine.org/news/media/releases/study_suggests_medical_errors_now_third_leading_cause_of_death_in_the_us

The Health Crisis 3

1. You can study this patented stem cell technology at www.lifewave.com. Additional patches for a variety of other health issues like sleeping are also available.

2. https://lcrhealth.com/active-stem/

* * *

Covid-19 Health Protocols

1. https://www.cdc.gov VAERS - Vaccine Injury Database

2. For a more detailed discussion and comparison of the two disease theories, go to https://factnest.com/health/disease-theories-germ-theory-vs-terrain-theory/

3. To study or learn more about the terrain theory, view the movies and information at - https://www.terrainthefilm.com

4. https://www.autismparentingmagazine.com/autism-statistics/

5. https://aidsrestherapy.biomedcentral.com/articles/10.1186/1742-6405-8-14

6. https://www.health.harvard.edu/mental-health/the-power-of-the-placebo-effect (As presented online 5/21/20)

7. https://www.sciencefocus.com/the-human-body/do-different-medicines-work-for-everyone/

8. https://www.wordnik.com/words/nocebo

9. Capitalized pronouns refer to God Almighty.

10. https://livelovefruit.com/how-your-body-rebuilds-itself-in-less-than-365-days/

11. All of the covid protocols mentioned here are subject to change. Do your research for the latest updates for Dr. Cheng and other doctors. The information provided here is what the author currently has on hand. Of particular note is the common elements of different protocols such as Vitamins D and C.

12. https://deerootsathome.com/dr-bryan-ardis-gives-life-saving-protocol-here/

13. https://brandnewtube.com/watch/disease-prevention-cocktail-dr-bryan-ardis_Li852fEIOu6Lpmq.html

Honesty, I Really Know Better!

1. In this context, paradigm means a level of achievement you have reached, which is represented by all your habits and current status in life. When you want to reach a new paradigm for your life, it means you will have to adopt new ways of living and new habits to get you there.

Focus On What You Can Control

1. New King James Bible

2. Today's English Version Bible

3. A teaching of R.H. Schuller and his Hour Of Power Ministry to lift your troubles up to God in prayer and simultaneously to downplay the importance of your earthly troubles or trials.

4. "Positive Thinking" was published by author Norman Vincent Peale in the mid 20th Century. His theological friend, Robert H. Schuller, picked up and later published the book "Possibility Thinking." Both books are excellent and reveal the power of your mind to help you move forward in life. This is especially true if you are in the midst of a crisis like a doctor's death diagnosis.

5. Low-cost professional courses are online for almost every topic you can think of at Udemy. It's a great way to improve your skills and get educated at your own pace, on your own time, and with your own financial budget. http://www.udemy.com

Exploring The Health Sandbox

1. http://www.ctfamily.org/hospice-patients-who-get-better/

2. https://www.vitas.com/hospice-and-palliative-care-basics/about-hospice-care/what-happens-if-i-get-better-while-in-hospice-care

The Sandbox Text

1. https://healingals.org/healedhealing-pals/

* * *

Self-Care Observations

1. http://edwardtheapostle.org

2. https://www.healthline.com/health/what-does-the-appendix-do#function

3. www.lifewave.com

4. https://www.youtube.com/watch?v=QeYMduufa-E. You can also search on G. Edward Griffin or his book *The World Without Cancer*.

5. You can buy apricot seed and other health supplies at this link https://www.rawfoodandvitamins.com

6. https://www.verywellhealth.com/what-is-fascia-5079645

7. A damaged LES valve is discussed at https://salgi.org/facts/heartburn/les/

8. https://gastrodigestivesystem.com/stomach/low-stomach-acid-symptoms

9. https://www.healthline.com/nutrition/19-best-prebiotic-foods#1.-Chicory-root

10. Biologist and author Bruce H. Lipton states we have 50 trillion cells in the body in his video teachings. The 380 trillion microorganisms was associated with the 100 trillion cell number from another source.

11. https://www.cdc.gov/cdiff/what-is.html

12. https://exploringyourmind.com/brain-microbiome-gut-bacteria-human-brain/

13. https://www.heartmath.org/our-heart-brain/

14. https://thebestbrainpossible.com/the-facts-you-need-to-know-about-fat-and-your-brain-health/

15. https://www.healthydirections.com/products/vision-health/vision-essentials-gold

16. https://www.marketcircle.com

17. https://healthifybody.com/amino-acid-list.html

18. https://www.sunchlorellausa.com

19. https://www.vitacost.com/vitacost-synergy-super-daily-enzymes

20. https://whatsgood.vitaminshoppe.com/nutrients-for-energy/

21.   https://www.verywellhealth.com/gaba-5095143

22.   https://www.healthline.com/health/l-theanine

Death Vs. Healing

1.   https://etactics.com/blog/medical-error-statistics

2.   https://www.hopkinsmedicine.org/news/media/releases/study_suggests_medical_errors_now_third_leading_cause_of_death_in_the_us

3.   https://www.mentalfloss.com/article/24149/how-scurvy-was-cured-then-cure-was-lost

4.   https://psychcentral.com/blog/the-surprising-history-of-the-lobotomy

5.   https://creativedestructionmedia.com/opinion/2022/04/12/why-i-no-longer-trust-doctors-or-hospitals/

Healing Secrets & Tips

1.   https://pubmed.ncbi.nlm.nih.gov/34264892/

2.   Psalms 90:10

3.   https://www.uchicagomedicine.org/forefront/cancer-articles/prostate-cancer-are-psa-blood-tests-reliable

62 Nutraceutical Secrets

1.   http://orthomolecular.org/nutrients/c.html

2.   http://www.orthomolecular.com/?ctr=supplement&act=show&id=18

3.   http://www.orthomolecular.com/?ctr=supplement

About The Author

Edward G. Palmer has studied alternative health issues for over 50 years. He took his first comprehensive multivitamin at the age of 25 in 1971. Already in excellent health and with plenty of energy, Ed was surprised that this multivitamin enhanced his health and vitality in a way that he could not deny. That experience became the foundation of a life long experience using vitamins and other nutraceuticals such as herbs to enhance his health. Ed quickly came to the conclusion that he could not bet his health on being able to eat well. Instead, Ed decided he would eat the best he could but would bet his overall health on supplementation with nutraceuticals. This book explains the lessons Ed learned about alternative health and living a long and healthy life. The story of how he came to take his first high-quality multivitamin is told in this book.

Other books by this author may be found online at the publisher's website at www.jvedpublishing.org.

Author Information

Edward G. Palmer

13570 Grove Drive #361

Maple Grove MN 55311

http://www.thedoctorsdeathdiagnosis.com

Publisher Information

JVED Publishing

13570 Grove Drive #361

Maple Grove MN 55311

http://www.jvedpublishing.org

A Companion Healing Book

Get a spiritual book on healing at

http://www.godandhealing.org

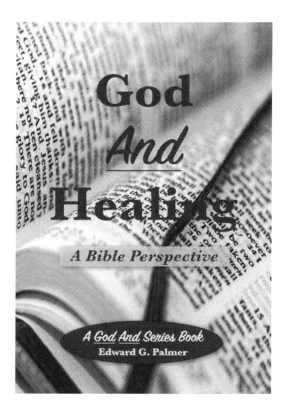

Get the Bible's Perspective on healing!

The Doctor's Death Diagnosis

Self Care, Your Health, And Healing Secrets

Self-care advice can give you hope and turn your death diagnosis around. Author Edward G. Palmer shares 50-years of alternative health and longevity studies, self-care discoveries, and low-cost healing secrets. Although traditional medicine has its place, it can become an expensive nightmare. You can enjoy remarkable health by thinking outside the box of conventional medicine and its methods. This book will teach you another way to look at health and healing; and how to approach it more cost-effectively.

JVED Publishing
13570 Grove Drive #361
Maple Grove MN 55311

9 780976 883395